Mammals

TIME LIFE Student Library

Mammals

Time-Life Books   Alexandria, Virginia

Table of Contents

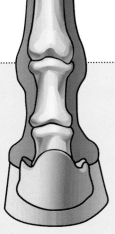

The Animal Kingdom

Life on earth exists in many forms, with some 9 to 10 million known species of animals and probably many more to be discovered. To organize all these creatures, scientists developed a system of classification that divides them into groups of related animals. This system is like a funnel, broad at the top and narrow at the bottom. The kingdom, the most general category, is broken down into groups called phyla, the phyla are subdivided into classes, and so on down to the most specific category, the species.

The chart below displays the great diversity within the animal kingdom, which is divided into vertebrates—animals with a backbone—and invertebrates—animals without a backbone.

Method of Classification

A quick way to remember the sequence of classification below is with the mnemonic "King Philip Cries Out For Good Soup." The first letter of each word is a clue to what comes next.
If you wanted to classify a lion, for example, it would look like this:

Kingdom	Animals
Phylum	Chordates
Class	Mammals
Order	Carnivores
Family	Cats
Genus	Large Cats
Species	Lion

Crustaceans

Crabs, lobsters, and barnacles are crustaceans. Most of the 40,000 different species are found in the sea. Their bodies are protected by a hard outer casing called an exoskeleton. They have jointed legs, and most breathe with gills.

Annelids

The more than 8,700 earthworms and other annelids are simple in structure: They have a head, a long, segmented body, and a digestive tract.

Mollusks

Most of the 100,000 species of mollusks live in the ocean and protect their soft bodies with a hard, external shell. Clams and snails are examples of mollusks.

◀ Invertebrates

Insects

Scientists know of 800,000 insect species but estimate that 30 million may exist. They include butterflies, grasshoppers, and ants. Like crustaceans, insects have an exoskeleton and jointed legs; most are terrestrial.

Lower Invertebrates

The lower invertebrates are the simplest animals. They include many phyla and classes of headless creatures like jellyfish, coral, sponges, and microscopic single-celled animals.

Vertebrates ▶

Amphibians

Frogs, salamanders, and other amphibians evolved from fishes more than 350 million years ago. Most of the 4,300 species live on land, but breed in water. Their skin is soft, without scales, and they are cold-blooded.

Reptiles

Crocodiles, lizards, snakes, and turtles are part of some 6,100 species of reptiles. They evolved from amphibians about 300 million years ago and have dry, scaly skin. Reptiles are cold-blooded.

Mammals

Mammals are one of the most successful groups in the animal kingdom. They evolved from reptiles about 200 million years ago and can now be found in almost every habitat, from the desert to the rain forest and from the deep sea to the mountaintops. Even so, mammals make up only a small percentage of all animals. There are about 4,500 species of mammals in the world; all are warm-blooded, meaning they maintain a constant body temperature, even when it is hotter or colder around them.

Birds

Birds are the only animals with feathers. The 9,000 species evolved from reptiles about 140 million years ago. Most birds can fly; they breathe with lungs and lay eggs with hard, waterproof shells. Like mammals, they are warm-blooded.

Fishes

About 540 million years ago, fishes evolved from the invertebrates. They live in water, absorbing oxygen through gills, and are cold-blooded, meaning they do not maintain a constant body temperature. Their bodies are covered with scales, and they use fins to swim. The 22,000 species of fish alive today include salmon, sharks, electric eel, and goldfish.

What Is a **Mammal?**

Mammals come in all shapes and sizes, and sometimes it's hard to see what they have in common. One characteristic shared by all 4,500 species is the feature for which they are named: mammary glands. The females have special glands that produce nutrient-rich milk for their young. Other attributes are hair, lungs to breathe with, and backbones.

They are divided into three main categories that re-flect the way the young develop: monotremes (*pages* 106-107), marsupials (*pages* 102-105), and placentals. The placental group is the largest category of mammals. The young develop inside the mother, attached to a placenta—a special organ that develops in the mother's womb and supplies the young with food and oxygen. The chart below shows the orders that make up the class Mammalia and gives examples of the kinds of animals found in each order.

Monotremata		Marsupialia		Insectivora		Macroscelidea	
Platypus		Koala	Wombat	Hedgehog	Tenrec	Elephant Shrew	
Short-nosed Echidna		Kangaroo	Bandicoot	Shrew	Solenodon		
Long-nosed Echidna		Opossum	Wallaby	Mole			

Dermoptera		Chiroptera		Scandentia		Primates	
		Fruit-eating Bat		Tree Shrew		Potto	Gibbon
Flying		Vampire Bat				Lemur	Gorilla
Lemur		Flower-feeding Bat				Monkey	Chimpanzee

Xenarthra/Pholidota		Lagomorpha		Rodentia		Cetacea	
Anteater	Armadillo	Rabbit	Pika	Porcupine	Hamster	Dolphin	Blue Whale
Sloth	Pangolin	Hare		Beaver	Jerboa	Porpoise	Right Whale
Silky Anteater				Squirrel	Capybara	Narwhal	Beluga

Carnivora		Pinnipedia		Tubulidentata		Proboscidea	
Cat	Bear	Walrus	Fur Seal	Aardvark		African and	
Wolf	Skunk	Sea Lion	Earless Seal			Indian	
Raccoon	Hyena					Elephants	

Hyracoidea		Sirenia		Perissodactyla		Artiodactyla	
Hyrax		Manatee		Zebra	Tapir	Giraffe	Deer
		Dugong		Horse	Donkey	Hippo	Pig
				Rhinoceros		Camel	Bison

In the Nursery

A lioness watches protectively as her cubs are nursing. Like all newborn mammals, lion cubs get their nourishment from their mother's milk. They will nurse for about seven months. During that time the young learn the lessons that will help them survive on their own.

Elephants

Elephants are the heavyweight champions of land mammals. They often stand more than 3 m (10 ft.) tall and weigh up to 6,800 kg (15,000 lbs.). That's taller than a basketball hoop and heavier than five cars. Even if elephants weren't so big, they would stand out because of their trunk. The trunk is like a nose, hand, and drinking straw rolled into one. Since this special nose is 1.8 m (6 ft.) long, elephants can eat both grass from the ground and leaves from trees. This is important because elephants need about 230 kg (500 lbs.) of food a day.

Their great size and strength protect elephants from all **predators,** except one: the human poacher. Humans have brought elephants to the brink of extinction by hunting them for their valuable ivory tusks.

Where in the World?

Elephants live in Africa and Asia.

Fast FACTS

Name Elephant

Number of Species 2

Family Elephantidae

Order Proboscidea

Shoulder Height 160-400 cm (5.2-13 ft.)

Weight at Maturity 2,400-7.5 kg (5,291-16,535 lbs.)

Distribution Africa (south of the Sahara), Southeast Asia

Habitat Savannas, plains, forests, wet marshes, semideserts

Food Chiefly grasses; also fruits, leaves, roots, twigs, bark

Social Structure In Africa, herds of maternal families, mature males in own groups, old bulls sometimes solitary; in Asia, herds of several maternal families, bulls usually solitary

Gestation Period 22 months

No. of Young per Pregnancy 1

Weight at Birth 60-135 kg (130-280 lbs.)

Longevity About 70 years

Conservation Status Endangered; hunted for their ivory tusks

Elephant herds are led by the oldest female, called the matriarch. Females stay with the herd their entire life. Males leave the herd around 14 years of age, often living alone or forming small groups of their own.

Sunblock: A young calf seeks shade from the blazing sun under its mother.

Let's Compare

African

Asian

Ears make the difference: There are only two species of elephants—the Asian and the African. They are easy to tell apart. Asian elephants have smaller ears and two "bumps" on their forehead. They also have smaller tusks; in fact, the females often don't have any tusks. The Asian elephants don't grow as large as their African cousins, and they have only one fingerlike projection on the end of their trunk instead of two.

Both species are intelligent, but the Asian elephants are easier to train. They are the ones you can see lifting and hauling loads, leading parades, and working in places where strength and sure-footedness are needed.

Prehistoric Woolly Mammoth

More than 40,000 years ago the woolly mammoth roamed the arctic regions of Europe, Asia, and western North America. This long-haired early ancestor of the elephant family became extinct some 8,000 years ago.

Elephants Close up

Despite their enormous size, elephants are among the most trainable animals. They have worked with humans for centuries. Their intelligence and sociable nature make them easy to tame.

Before there were cars, trains, and tanks, elephants served in Asia and Africa as royal transportation, as freight carriers, and in warfare. Even today elephants in Asia work in construction and march in parades.

These gentle giants can be extremely dangerous, though, especially the males. Solitary strays called rogues, who have not been able to find a mate or a group of other males to join, have at times become so enraged that they have trampled entire villages in Africa.

Most of the time humans and elephants have gotten along well together. It is respect for both the elephant's intelligence and its frightening power that makes it an honored beast for people in Africa and Asia. In India elephants are revered in the form of a statue of a man with an elephant's head, representing the Hindu god Ganesh, who helps people make the right decisions.

More than 40,000 muscles and tendons in an elephant's trunk make it flexible enough to pick up a single stem or a peanut with its fingerlike projections.

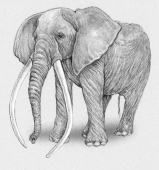

The thousands of muscles make the trunk incredibly strong, too—strong enough to do heavy lifting in logging and construction.

Ahmed, the African elephant, had the longest tusks ever at 3 m (10 ft.). Elephants use their tusks as lifters and levers and as shovels to dig for water.

When Bulls Collide

The only animal not afraid to take on an elephant is another elephant. Fights among elephants are rare and usually occur between two bulls competing for the attention of a female. Battles between these large beasts are earth-shaking and violent. Often one of the bulls is killed. Young male elephants usually gather in bachelor groups, where they can practice fighting to test their strength. These contests end when the loser gives up and simply walks away.

Six-Ton Submarine

Elephants love water, and they are great swimmers *(above)*. They have been known to swim 48 km (30 mi.) at a time. Their trunk comes in handy as a snorkel, and also as a hose *(right)* for cooling off in the scorching African heat.

Tools of War and Labor

In the third century B.C.
General Hannibal, of the African city-state Carthage, trained an army of elephants for war against the Roman Empire. The elephants were no match, however, for the superior Roman forces. Many perished when crossing the snowy mountain passes of the Alps *(right)*.

In India elephants are vital to the logging industry. The sure-footed beasts can navigate muddy hills better than bulldozers and trucks can.

What Are Hoofed Mammals?

Hoofed mammals, or **ungulates,** are mammals that have large sheaths called hoofs covering their toes. Hoofs are like giant fingernails; they are also made of the same substance, called **keratin.** This feature allows many different mammals to be grouped into two scientific orders: odd-toed ungulates, the Perissodactyla, and even-toed ones, the Artiodactyla.

There are only three living families of odd-toed ungulates: horses (including zebras), rhinoceroses, and tapirs. These three families comprise 15 different species of mammals. Even-toed ungulates are a much larger lot; they include more than 160 species grouped into nine families. Camels, pigs, and hippopotamuses all have hoofs with an even number of toes. That is also true for all mammals that have antlers or horns: giraffes, deer, antelopes, gazelles, sheep, goats, and cattle, such as the stampeding buffalo at right.

Hoofed mammals tend to travel in herds. And all hoofed mammals, whether they have an odd or an even number of toes, are almost exclusively plant eaters.

Even-toed

Even-toed ungulates have either two toes like camels *(left)* and deer *(middle)*, or four toes like hippos *(right)*.

Odd-toed

Odd-toed ungulates have either one toe like horses and zebras *(left)*, or three toes like rhinos *(right)*.

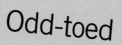

Cloven-hoofed

Cloven-hoofed means a hoof split in two—like the feet of deer and goats. They actually have two hoofs on two different toes, not one hoof split in half. The word "cloven-hoofed" has become a colorful term meaning "evil," based on ancient illustrations showing the devil with goat legs.

Tapir: Odd Man Out

The funny-nosed tapir isn't slender like a horse, or strong like a rhino, but is related to both because of its odd number of toes. Tapirs live in the dense forests of Central and South America and Malaysia, and they would rather swim than run.

Zebras Horses of a Different Stripe

In a way a zebra is simply a horse with stripes. Horses, zebras, and donkeys all belong to the same family, called Equidae. Zebras are one of the world's only true wild horses, meaning they have never been tamed by humans.

Some scientists think the unusual stripes act as **camouflage** for zebras in the wide-open African plains. When zebras run, the blur of stripes may confuse the **predators.** Others maintain that the stripes serve only as identification. It's true, the predators have no trouble spotting the zebras; they are the prey of choice for lions, leopards, and hyenas. For this reason zebras are very skittish. The slightest noise around a watering hole will send a whole herd scrambling for safety.

Where in the World?

Zebras live in Africa.

Fast FACTS

Name Zebra

Number of Species 3

Family Equidae

Order Perissodactyla

Shoulder Height 120-160 cm (4-5.3 ft.)

Weight at Maturity 300-450 kg (660-990 lbs.)

Distribution Eastern, central, southern Africa (south of the Sahara)

Habitat Plains, savannas, and sometimes mountainous regions

Food Grasses

Social Structure Herds of 10-12 (migration herds may be huge); old males occasionally solitary

Gestation Period 11-13 months

No. of Young per Pregnancy 1

Weight at Birth 25-40 kg (55-88 lbs.)

Longevity 20 years

Conservation Status Burchell's zebra is the only species not threatened with extinction; all zebras are hunted for their skin; they often vie with domestic livestock for food and water

What Color Is a Zebra?

That's an easy one, right? It's black and white! But is a zebra a white animal with black stripes, or a black animal with white stripes? Depending on their own skin color, people tend to answer the question differently.

Flee or Fight

If this pregnant Grevy's zebra seems huge, it's because newborn zebra foals are unusually large— about twice as big proportionally as human babies— and they are much more developed.

The best way for a zebra to stay alive is to run from trouble in its special zigzag way. Zebras have narrow hoofs and long legs adapted for running fast. Sometimes, though, they have no choice but to fight. The zebra at right uses its hoofs to kick a black leopard and may use its sharp teeth to bite.

The question of a zebra's color isn't as simple as black and white. Zebras often start life off in a different color—usually a sort of rust or tawny brown, like the nursing foal above. A foal's familiar black and white markings appear at about four months of age.

Would **You** *Believe?*

At first glance all zebras look alike. But no two zebras are exactly the same. Just as each human has a unique set of fingerprints, each zebra has a striped pattern all its own. Zebras recognize one another by their special markings.

Zebra stripes are as unique as your fingerprints.

Horses Tame and Fiery Breeds

Pony

The ponies' small size makes them ideal for children to ride on.

Unlike zebras, horses have been **domesticated**—tamed and bred by humans—for more than 5,000 years. They have served humans ever since as transport, in the hunt, and in war. The last wild horses were Przewalski's horses, a breed discovered only in 1879 in the steppes of central Asia. Today even they live only on preserves and in zoos.

All 180 horse breeds can be separated into three main groups: ponies, and light and heavy horses. Ponies are the smallest ones—shorter than 14.2 hands, or 144 cm (57 in.)—and were once used to haul wagons in small spaces, like coal mines. Light horses are sleek and fast; they are the horses of the Old West, thoroughbred racing, and recreational riding. Heavy horses, such as the Clydesdales, were bred as draft, or pulling, horses. The term "horsepower" comes from these breeds.

Light Horse

Light horses, such as these thoroughbred racers, are among the world's fastest mammals.

Where in the World?

Horses live on all continents except Antarctica.

Fast FACTS

Name Horse

Number of Species 1

Family Equidae

Order Perissodactyla

Shoulder Height 100-168 cm (3-5.5 ft.)

Weight at Maturity 175-930 kg (385-2,050 lbs.)

Distribution Found throughout the world due to reintroduction by man

Habitat Grassy or shrubby terrain

Food Mainly grass

Social Structure Herds

Gestation Period 11-13 months

No. of Young per Pregnancy Usually 1

Weight at Birth 25-45 kg (55-99 lbs.)

Longevity 25-30 years

Conservation Status Domestic breeds are plentiful; only one wild subspecies, Przewalski's horse, survives—a few of this breed may still occur in the wild in Mongolia and western China, and about 700 live in zoos

Heavy Horse

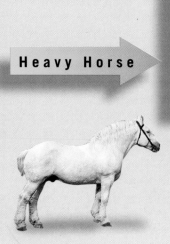

Heavy horses are still used as draft horses in farm and logging work because of their strength.

White stallions of Galicia, Spain, battle one another with pounding hoofs and flying manes during a roundup.

Relatives

DONKEY

Donkeys—horses' close relatives—are the domesticated version of the African wild ass. They are smaller and stockier than light horses and have wider feet. Donkeys are mainly used as work animals. They are also crossbred with horses to make mules—the farm animal known for its stubbornness.

Would **You** *Believe?*

Horses run on their fingertips.

All horses have just one toe on each foot. The bone structure is similar to a human hand with only the middle finger remaining so that horses are really running only on their middle fingers.

Rhinos Fleet-footed Runners

Let's **Compare**

Rhinos are among the most feared animals in the world. If you weighed 3,600 kg (7,900 lbs.), had sharp horns on your nose, and a reputation for being mean, people would be afraid of you, too.

These heavy, horned "tanks" of Africa and Asia are, in fact, quite timid. Their well-known reputation for charging may stem from poor eyesight. They can't tell friend or foe from a distance, so they charge everything in their way just to be safe. Rhinoceroses have even been seen charging trees and rocks.

Many other animals have horns, but only the rhinoceros sports them on its nose. African rhinoceroses have two horns, and Asians (except the Sumatran rhino) have one. Some people think the myth of the unicorn came in part from descriptions of the one-horned Asian rhinos. All rhinos use their horns to defend their young from **predators.**

Where in the World?

Rhinos live in Africa and Asia.

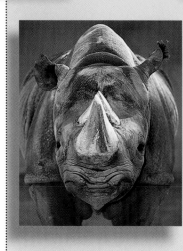

Black Rhino

Black rhinos, which aren't really black but gray, have a finger-like projection on their upper lip, like the end of an elephant's trunk. It lets them grab leaves from trees and shrubs.

White Rhino

White rhinos have a square upper lip, indicating that they mainly eat grass. They aren't really white—they too are gray. Their name comes from the South African word "wijd," meaning wide, for wide lip.

Hairy Rhino

The Sumatran rhino is the only rhino with much hair on its body—hence its nickname, the "hairy rhino." It is the smallest of all rhinos and is the only Asian species with two horns.

Fast FACTS

Name Rhinoceros

Number of Species 5

Family Rhinocerotidae

Order Perissodactyla

Shoulder Height 160-200 cm (5-6.5 ft.)

Weight at Maturity 1,000-3,600 kg (2,200-7,900 lbs.)

Distribution Africa and eastern Asia (including Sumatra, Java, and Borneo)

Habitat Savannas, shrubby regions, and dense forests

Food Grass or branches

Social Structure Mother and young offspring stay together; otherwise, generally solitary

Gestation Period 15-16 months

No. of Young per Pregnancy 1

Weight at Birth 25-80 kg (55-176 lbs.)

Longevity 40-50 years

Conservation Status Endangered; all species rare or approaching rarity or extinction

Horn Robbers

Rhinos have become **endangered** because of a great demand for their valuable horns. For centuries these horns have been ground into a powder as an ingredient in Asian folk medicines. But the greatest demand comes from the men of Yemen, a country in the Middle East. The men use the horns to make handles for ceremonial daggers *(left)*. At right is Chitwan, a newborn Asian rhino successfully bred in captivity at the National Zoological Park in Washington, D.C. —one way to try and preserve the rare species.

Rhino on a Roll

Don't let the massive body and stocky legs of this great Indian rhino fool you. Charging rhinos have been clocked at 45 km/h (28 mph)—at least twice as fast as you can run.

Hippos River Horses of Africa

The ancient Greeks called hippopotamuses "river horses" because they spend so much time in the water. On a normal day these rotund beasts will spend 18 hours in a mudhole, emerging at night only to graze. Hippos are well suited for life on land and in water. Their nostrils, eyes, and ears are on top of their head, like a frog's, so they can sit almost submerged and still see and breathe. Their skin secretes a pinkish **mucus** to help them retain moisture on land—a feature that makes hippos look as if they are sweating blood. Hippo babies can even swim before they can walk, and they nurse underwater. Despite being larger than any land mammal except elephants and rhinos, hippos seem harmless because of their plump figures. In reality they are one of the most dangerous animals in the world. They topple boats and bite the boaters to death, killing more people than lions do.

Where in the World?

Hippos can be found in Africa.

A four-ton hippo moves effortlessly underwater by walking on the bottom. The visible scars on its face are signs of combat.

What's Symbiosis?

Symbiosis means that two very different organisms benefit from living with each other. Hippos don't like insects biting them, so they allow cattle egrets to sit on their backs and pick off the insects. The birds eat the insects, and both animals are better off.

Fast FACTS

Name Hippopotamus

Number of Species 1

Family Hippopotamidae

Order Artiodactyla

Shoulder Height 150-165 cm (4.9-5.4 ft.)

Weight at Maturity 1,000-4,000 kg (2,200-8,800 lbs.)

Distribution Sub-Saharan Africa

Habitat Rivers and lakes

Food Mainly grass

Social Structure Found singly, in pairs, in groups of 15, or sometimes in groups as large as 150

Gestation Period 7-8 months

No. of Young per Pregnancy 1, rarely 2

Weight at Birth 25-55 kg (55-121 lbs.)

Longevity About 41 years in the wild; 54 years in captivity

Conservation Status Mostly extinct or very rare but abundant in some protected areas; hunted for its flesh, fat, hide, and the superior ivory of its teeth

DOMESTIC PIG

Although they don't look alike, pigs and hippos are related. Pigs are smart and have a well-developed sense of smell. Some domestic pigs are trained by French farmers *(above)* to sniff out truffles—rare mushroomlike fungi growing underground that are expensive delicacies.

WARTHOG

The warthog, a wild African pig, gets its name from four wartlike lumps of tissue that protrude from the face of the male. When males engage in combat and strike with their tusks, the warts help protect them. At mealtime they drop on their wrists to graze on grass.

WILD BOAR

The European wild boar is the direct ancestor of **domesticated** pigs like the one at top. If they cannot hide from **predators** in dense vegetation, wild boars will attack any intruder with their tusks—including humans.

I Was There!

When Alan Root was taking photos of hippos in Garamba, Congo, a nation in central Africa, with the help of local guides, he soon learned what can happen when a bull is provoked. He began to photograph a group of submerged hippos, and "suddenly," he reported, "one hippo got my leg right in his mouth, so that the left-hand **canines** were slicing through the calf while my foot and ankle were between his right-hand molars. The hippo then shook me like a rat." Luckily for Root, his attacker lost interest and dropped him.

Camels Desert Voyagers

Fabulous Features!

Camels are vital to people who live in the deserts of Asia, Africa, and the Middle East. They can carry loads equal to their own weight, and they tolerate the extreme heat and cold of desert climates, which makes them valuable as beasts of burden. People of the desert make good use of camels in other ways: They drink the camel's milk, eat the meat, use the dung for fuel, and weave the hair into cloth.

It's true that camels can go for weeks without water. But it is a myth that they store water in their humps. The hump is where fat, a source of energy, is stored. When a camel has gone without food and water for a long time, the hump sags and leans to one side. Fortunately camels are energy conservers. They stand at an angle to the sun to keep from getting too hot. And they don't sweat as much as other mammals, reducing their need for water.

Where in the World?

Camels can be found in Africa, Asia, and Australia.

Eyes and nose: Camels have long eyelashes to keep sand out of their eyes. Besides a top and bottom eyelid, a third lid helps remove sand. Camels can shut their nostrils to keep sand from blowing in. Their nostrils drain into their mouth, so they can use their own mucus for moisture.

Long, thin legs and big, round feet—as wide as a dinner plate—allow camels to walk in soft sand without sinking in. To see how it works, try the experiment below.

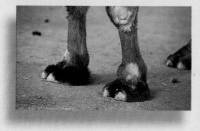

Try It!

Stick a pencil in a sandbox. It goes straight in, right? Now place a quarter under the pencil. The extra surface area keeps the pencil from sinking deep into the sand.

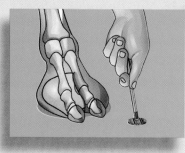

Fast FACTS

Name Camel

Number of Species 2

Family Camelidae

Order Artiodactyla

Shoulder Height 180-230 cm (6-7.5 ft.)

Weight at Maturity 300-690 kg (660-1,520 lbs.)

Distribution Domestic camels in northern Africa through central Asia to Mongolia; wild camels in Gobi Desert; feral population in deserts of central Australia

Habitat Deserts, steppes

Food Leaves, herbs, grasses

Social Structure Herds—either single-sex, or females and offspring led by a single male

Gestation Period 12-14 months

No. of Young per Pregnancy 1, rarely 2

Weight at Birth 37 kg (82 lbs.)

Longevity 30-40 years

Conservation Status Wild camels considered vulnerable or endangered; domestic camels plentiful

Let's Compare

There are two types of camels: the domesticated dromedary and the wild Bactrian of western China. To tell the difference, remember "D" is for Dromedary and "B" for Bactrian. Dromedaries have one hump, like a "D." Bactrians have two humps, like a "B."

Trot or Pace

T r o t

P a c e

Horses trot: They move their left front and right rear legs at the same time, and then move the opposite pair, as above, for a smooth ride.
Camels pace: They move both legs on the same side at one time, then the legs on the other side, causing them to roll from side to side.

Camels, whether wild or tame, move together in single file. When they travel with people—some camels carrying riders and others carrying loads—the line-up is called a caravan. The name "camel" may come from the ancient Arabic word "gamel," meaning "carrying a burden."

Llamas and Their Kin

Llamas, guanacos, alpacas, and vicuñas are all members of the same family as camels. They lack the distinctive humps of their more famous relatives. But like those desert voyagers, llamas and their kin are indispensable to the people who live in the rugged Andes mountain region of South America.

Llamas thrive as **domesticated** animals in mountains. Their blood is specially adapted to deal with reduced oxygen and freezing temperatures at high altitudes. And their cloven hoofs help make them good climbers, like sheep and goats. Local inhabitants use llamas mostly as pack animals in places where cars and trucks cannot go. They also use the animals' meat for food, their hides for leather goods, their dung for heating fuel, and their wool for clothing. Two species in particular—the alpaca and vicuña—are prized for their soft, luxurious wool.

Where in the World?

Llamas live in the Andes mountains of South America.

Fast FACTS

Name Llama

Number of Species 4

Family Camelidae

Order Artiodactyla

Shoulder Height 70-130 cm (2.3-4.3 ft.)

Weight at Maturity 35-155 kg (77-342 lbs.)

Distribution Andes region of western South America (Peru, Bolivia, Argentina, and Chile)

Habitat Dry, open country, often in mountains

Food Grasses and leaves

Social Structure Small herds with one male and several females

Gestation Period 11-12 months

No. of Young per Pregnancy 1, rarely 2

Weight at Birth 4-16 kg (9-35 lbs.)

Longevity 15-24 years

Conservation Status Llama being replaced by trucks and trains; guanaco and vicuña threatened by excessive hunting; alpaca bred for value of its fleece

Rite of Passage

An older male guanaco is attacking a younger one to drive him away from the herd. The young male will join a bachelor herd until he is ready to mate.

The Mighty Little Llama

The llamas' small size and slender build belie the fact that they can carry loads of up to 100 kg (220 lbs.). During the great Incan Empire, long before cars and machines existed, llamas were essential for mountain transportation. One historian said the Incan Empire stretched only as far as the llamas' territorial range.

Incan Idol

The Incas held llamas sacred. They fashioned images out of silver like the one above, thought to represent the white llama, symbol of royalty. And they decorated idols of their gods *(left)* with blankets of vicuña wool, which was considered too luxurious for common people.

Giraffes The Tallest of All

Giraffes are the tallest of all living land mammals. Males usually grow to about 5 m (17 ft.) in height, and the tallest giraffe ever towered at 5.8 m (19 ft.). Would you believe, then, that giraffes were not named for their height? "Giraffe" comes from an Arabic word meaning "the one that walks very fast." Since giraffes take strides of about 4.5 m (15 ft.), you would have to run just to keep up.

Their long necks allow giraffes to eat leaves from the treetops. In some parts of Africa the trees have been flattened by their nibbling. Giraffes also use their necks as weapons, swinging them at their foes like golf clubs *(right)*. But giraffes are timid and prefer to avoid trouble. They can spot danger kilometers away because of their height and keen vision. Giraffes can go for weeks without water. This keeps them away from watering holes where **predators** lurk.

Where in the World?

The giraffes' habitat is in Africa.

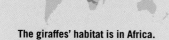

Head Rush

A special valve system regulates the flow of blood from the giraffes' heart to their head. When they bend down, valves in the jugular vein close, so the blood will not suddenly rush to their head at great pressure, which would cause them to pass out.

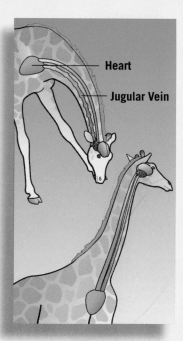

- Heart
- Jugular Vein

High Fashion

When the first giraffe was brought to Paris, France, in 1827, Parisians went wild for "giraffe style." Men started wearing coats patterned after the giraffe's spots. And women had their hair done up in a style resembling the giraffe's head.

Fast FACTS

Name Giraffe

Number of Species 1

Family Giraffidae

Order Artiodactyla

Shoulder Height 250-370 cm (8-12 ft.)

Weight at Maturity 550-1,930 kg (1,212-4,255 lbs.)

Distribution Africa (south of the Sahara)

Habitat Savannas

Food Leaves and fresh shoots

Social Structure Family groups or large herds

Gestation Period 15 months

No. of Young per Pregnancy 1, very rarely 2

Weight at Birth 47-70 kg (103-154 lbs.)

Longevity 26 years in the wild; 36 years in captivity

Conservation Status Severely endangered in West Africa; still common in East Africa

Relative

OKAPI

The okapi is a short relative of the giraffe. European scientists didn't even know this animal existed until 1901. At that time an English explorer named Sir Harry Johnston met a soldier in the Congo region, in Africa, who was wearing a shoulder strap made from okapi hide. It took several more years before the shy animal was seen alive by a European.

Giraffes are browsers, meaning they eat leaves off trees and shrubs rather than graze on grass. Their tongues, which are about 60 cm (2 ft.) long, help them strip leafy branches clean.

Deer Family
The Growth of Antlers

The first thing you notice about deer is their antlers. Some are huge, like the elk's, with lots of points, called tines. Some are small, like those of the pudu *(page 33)*. Only the male of each species grows antlers, except for the caribou. But antlers are what set deer apart—no other animal grows them.

A big rack of antlers is fierce-looking. Antlers' primary purpose, however, is a social one. Males, called bucks, with big antlers are more attractive to females, called does. Big antlers are a sign of good health, and does would rather mate with healthy bucks.

Unfortunately, big antlers are also prized by hunters. Even one of the few species without antlers—the musk deer—is hunted for its "musk," a scent used to make perfume. The main defense deer have against humans and other **predators** is their great speed running through forests.

Where in the World?

Deer live in most parts of the world.

Fast FACTS

Name Deer

Number of Species 45

Family Cervidae

Order Artiodactyla

Shoulder Height Shortest: pudu, 25-43 cm (10-17 in.); tallest: moose, 140-235 cm (4.5-7.7 ft.)

Weight at Maturity Pudu, 5.8-13.4 kg (12.7-30 lbs.); moose, 200-825 kg (440-1,819 lbs.)

Distribution Virtually worldwide except in central and southern Africa and Antarctica

Habitat Extremely varied, from forests to deserts to Arctic tundras

Food Grass, bark, twigs, young shoots, and leaves

Social Structure Usually in groups

Gestation Period 5-9 months

No. of Young per Pregnancy 1-2, sometimes 3-4

Weight at Birth 1-18 kg (2-40 lbs.)

Longevity 8-20 years

Conservation Status Many species are endangered; others are overbreeding and are agricultural and forest pests

Missing Parts

Little bony stumps, called pedicels, on the deer's forehead show where antlers have fallen off. A deer loses its antlers every winter and has to regrow them.

June

Throughout spring and summer the antlers grow. During this time they are covered with a thin, velvety skin. The velvet contains blood vessels that nourish the antlers.

September

Antlers are full-grown by the fall mating season. The deer shed their velvet by rubbing the antlers against a tree trunk. Some deer eat the velvet. Each year the antlers grow back one tine larger.

January

Once the mating season is over, usually between January and April, the deer's antlers simply fall off. They normally drop off one at a time. Some deer eat their newly shed antlers for the nutrients.

Moose Hangs Loose

This bull moose is beginning to shed its velvet in long, bloody strips. The huge palmated antlers (meaning "shaped like a hand") of a moose can weigh 36 kg (80 lbs.). Despite their size, moose are usually timid and solitary. Most of their time is spent eating from shrubs and trees and plants growing in water—they have to eat 20 kg (45 lbs.) of food a day. At times moose can be fierce. They have been known to attack trains, possibly mistaking them for rival bulls.

What Are Antlers For?

Fighting

Advancing with great power, a caribou is trying to push an attacking grizzly bear off balance and gore it. Deer mainly fight with each other during mating season, but they also wield their antlers to defend themselves against predators.

Cooling Off

In summer antlers provide a cooling system. They carry a supply of blood, which is cooled by the outside air before it recirculates through the body. When the antlers fall off, the blood shuts off.

Deer Family Close up

The deer family is one of the largest and most widespread families of mammals in the world. Deer probably originated in Asia. Now more than 40 species of deer roam every part of the world except central and southern Africa and Antarctica. They range in size from the moose, which stands 1.8 m (6 ft.) tall and weighs nearly a ton, to the pudu, which is only 30 cm (1 ft.) tall and weighs 7 kg (15 lbs.).

Like their fellow cloven-hoofed mammals, deer are mainly plant eaters. But deer are also a favorite meal of many predators, including humans, so stopping to browse is a hazard. Fortunately for them, deer are **ruminants.** Ruminants are plant-eating hoofed mammals that have three or four chambers in the stomach *(page 40)*. Their special stomachs allow ruminants to "chew their cud." That means they can eat grass or leaves in a hurry, then go off to safety, cough up the food, and rechew what they've already swallowed once. Besides deer, ruminants include camels, giraffes, antelopes and gazelles, cattle and buffalo, and sheep and goats.

Winner Takes All

A victorious male red deer lets out a mighty roar, announcing his dominance over the herd after prolonged battle with another male. He is surrounded by the females, called a harem. In the future he may have to defend his position against still other, younger bucks.

Head to Head

Two red deer bucks are locking antlers—a mating season ritual in which the males with the biggest antlers battle each other for control of the herd.

Dainty Deer

The pudu, native to South America, is small enough to be held by a child. The solitary animal is endangered; it has been hunted relentlessly, and its habitat is shrinking.

PUDU

Musk & Tusks

The musk deer lives in the dense forests of Southeast Asia, where antlers would get in the way. Instead of antlers, it has long tusklike teeth, called **canines.**

MUSK DEER

Hiding Spots

The white spots on the coat of a newborn red deer help hide the fawn in tall grass.

Pretty Quick

The graceful roe deer is Europe's most common deer species. It is the fastest wild mammal in Britain and, like the American white-tailed deer, is a favorite of hunters.

ROE DEER

Caribou on the Long Tre

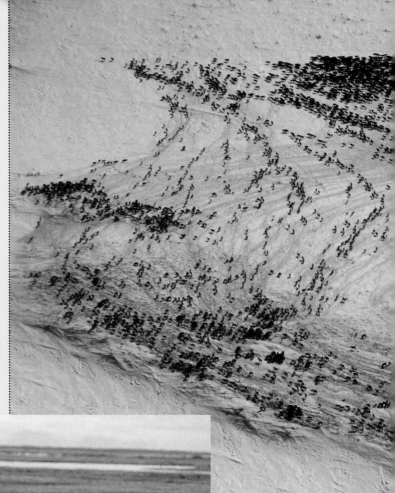

Every year caribou, which live in the Arctic regions of the world, travel up to 1,500 km (900 mi.) south to their winter feeding grounds. There they feed on twigs and lichens. When spring comes, they head back north to browse on new leaves and shrubs. The young are born along the way in late May and June.

Caribou travel in large herds—some totaling more than 100,000 animals—and their annual march can be heard for miles around because of an unusual clicking sound made by the tendons in their feet.

Caribou are well equipped for their rugged Arctic terrain. Their coats, which consist of long, stiff guard hairs growing over a soft, curly undercoat, get longer and thicker as winter approaches. And they are able to allow the temperature in their legs and feet to drop so they can conserve heat in the rest of their body.

What's Migration?

Some animals in the far north travel south when winter comes to find warmer weather and plenty of food. In the spring they return to their summer feeding grounds. For many animals this involves a long journey called migration. Birds are the best-known long-distance travelers, but insects, fish, and even some mammals undertake these journeys.

Certain bats travel north in the spring to follow flying insects. With colder weather and fewer insects, they return to their winter caves in the south. Many of the larger whales *(pages 110-113)* travel north when the water turns warm and south again for the winter.

No land mammal, though, travels as far in a single year as the caribou.

Large migrating herds, such as the one above, have been described as a "river of caribou," because they move along in a steady stream. They are a welcome sight to many Arctic natives. Caribou are primary sources of meat and hides for people who live in the remote villages of Alaska and Canada.

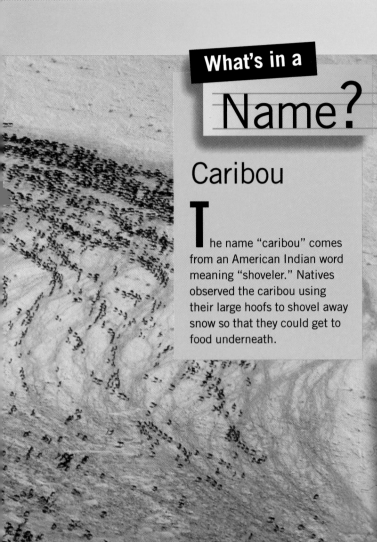

What's in a Name?

Caribou

The name "caribou" comes from an American Indian word meaning "shoveler." Natives observed the caribou using their large hoofs to shovel away snow so that they could get to food underneath.

Fabulous Features!

Nature's Snowshoes

Caribou feet are broad to allow them to walk on soft snow. During winter the foot pads shrink, exposing more of the hoof, to provide better traction on ice. Their rear dewclaws, which do not reach the ground on other hoofed mammals, are also well-developed for traction.

Santa's Sleigh Drivers

The European caribou are called reindeer. And yes, they really do live near the North Pole, where they have been trained to pull sleighs for people living in the north of Norway, Sweden, and Finland. Unlike Rudolph of the song, the only reason a real reindeer would have a red nose is from the cold—temperatures where they live can drop to 50° C (58° F) below zero.

Born to Run

Caribou calves, which are born during migration, weigh about 6 kg (13 lbs.) at birth. Yet after only 24 hours they can not only walk but even outrun a person.

Antelopes and Gazelles

Antelopes and gazelles are usually noticed for their horns, which come in unusual shapes. Though a few antelopes live in Asia, most can be found leaping and bounding on the open plains of Africa. There they compete with other mammals for grazing territory, while using their speed to avoid becoming a meal for cheetahs, lions, and hyenas.

One antelope-like creature is in a league of its own. The superfast pronghorn antelope of North America, pictured at right, is not, scientifically, an antelope, despite its name and the strong resemblance. Its forward-pointing prongs, unlike true horns, are shed annually. Able to run at 80 km/h (50 mph), it is faster than any mammal other than the cheetah. And unlike the cheetah, which runs only in short spurts, the pronghorn can sustain that speed for several miles.

PRONGHORN

Where in the World?

Pronghorn antelopes live in North America and Mexico.

Fast FACTS

Name Pronghorn antelope

Number of Species 1

Family Antilocapridae

Order Artiodactyla

Shoulder Height 81-104 cm (2.7-3.4 ft.)

Weight at Maturity 36-70 kg (79-154 lbs.)

Distribution North America

Habitat Grasslands and deserts

Food Herbs and grasses; also leafy shrubs, cacti, and other plants

Social Structure During fall and winter, form large, loose herds; otherwise groups are smaller and segregated by sex

Gestation Period 8.5 months

No. of Young per Pregnancy 1-2, rarely 3

Weight at Birth 2-4 kg (4.4-8.8 lbs.)

Longevity 12 years in captivity

Conservation Status Populations recovering from past overhunting; still threatened or endangered in parts of the U.S. and Mexico

Would You Believe?

Stand-Up Guy

The gerenuk of Africa, which browses on acacia trees, stands on its hind legs to get the choicest leaves. Other gazelles and even deer can rear up on their hind legs. But the gerenuk can stand unsupported like this and even walk around.

Backscratchers

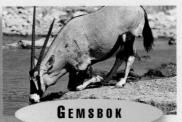

GEMSBOK

When a gemsbok lowers its head with its horns pointing forward, its long, straight horns serve as dangerous weapons. The silver, black, and white animal is one of the largest African antelopes.

Spiraling Horns

The greater kudu sports some of the most magnificent horns in nature. They spiral elegantly from its head to a length of up to 1.8 m (6 ft.)—longer than the kudu's entire body.

KUDU

Leapers

Antelopes and gazelles are great leapers, as the aptly-named springbok demonstrates. The springbok can jump as high as 3 m (10 ft.) off the ground. This is known as pronging, a signal that a predator has been seen.

SPRINGBOK

Let's **Compare**

Antlers

Horns

Antlers, which occur only on deer, are solid bone structures that grow and fall off each year. Except for caribou, where both sexes sport antlers, only male deer have antlers. Horns, though, are usually grown by both male and female animals, and are permanent. They consist of a sheath of **keratin**—like hoofs—covering a bony core and continue to grow through adulthood.

Tiny Spikes

Dik-diks get their name from the sound they make. The hare-size antelopes, with little more than sprigs for horns, are so small they are even preyed upon by large birds, besides the usual predators. These shy animals hide in dense shrubbery, on which they feed.

DIK-DIK

Make Way for Buffalo

W hen North America was first settled, some 50 million bison were roaming the continent's prairies and forests. "The moving multitude...darkened the whole plains," wrote the Western explorers Lewis and Clark. The vast herds of these massive, humpbacked beasts moved slowly most of the time, grazing on prairie grasses. But a loud thunderclap could instantly send the herd into one of their legendary, deadly stampedes.

European settlers, who mistakenly called the American bison "buffalo," nearly wiped out the bison by the end of the 19th century. Pioneers hunted them for sport and to weaken the American Indians. Eliminating bison robbed them of their main source of food and clothing, as well as a sacred animal vital to their spiritual life. Thanks to conservation efforts, the bison has made a comeback.

Where in the World?

American bison roam North America.

Let's Compare

American Bison

European Bison

There are two species of bison: American and European. Both have shaggy brown coats and short, upturned horns. But European bison have longer legs and lack the large, muscular hump of their American cousin. European bison, which were also hunted mightily, no longer exist in the wild, but still live in preserves in Eastern Europe.

The Buffalo Hunters

This 19th-century print by Currier & Ives depicts the slaughter of bison in the American West after the Civil War. Legendary hunters like Buffalo Bill Cody wiped out huge numbers of bison. Cody himself once bragged about killing 4,280 buffalo in an 18-month period.

Fast FACTS

Name American Bison

Number of Species 1

Family Bovidae

Order Artiodactyla

Shoulder Height 150-200 cm (5-6.5 ft.)

Weight at Maturity 350-1,000 kg (772-2,205 lbs.)

Distribution North America

Habitat Prairies, aspen parkland, open woodland

Food Prairie herbs and grasses; in winter, also mosses and lichens

Social Structure Range from small family herd to herd of thousands

Gestation Period 9-9.5 months

No. of Young per Pregnancy 1, rarely 2

Weight at Birth 15-30 kg (33-66 lbs.)

Longevity 18-22 years

Conservation Status Plains buffalo common, but few are truly wild, having descended from captive stock; Canada's woodland buffalo endangered

The birth of Miracle in 1994—the first true female white buffalo born this century—was seen by Native Americans as the fulfillment of the prophecy of Black Elk, a Sioux holy man of the 1800s. He said White Buffalo Calf Woman would return in seven generations to restore peace to a troubled world.

Return of the White Buffalo Calf

A dancer dresses as White Buffalo Calf Woman for an annual American Indian ceremony. Legend says that a maiden brought a sacred pipe to the Lakota Sioux centuries ago, then disappeared in the form of a white buffalo calf, promising to return one day.

Buffalo Close up

True buffalo are native to Africa and Asia. They are similar in size to bison, but they have shorter coats and longer, more curved horns. The Cape buffalo lives on the grassy plains of Africa and is wild. It has a reputation for being dangerous and has no qualms about attacking a lion with its long horns. The water buffalo of Asia, by contrast, was domesticated thousands of years ago. It is a valuable farm animal in the river valleys.

Bovines (cattlelike mammals, which include the yak, the musk oxen, and the other animals shown on these pages) are social animals and usually travel in herds. Most live in wide-open grasslands, though some inhabit forests and mountain areas. Both males and females grow horns. And all are grazers, using their teeth to pull up grass by its roots rather than bite off the ends, as horses do. In order to digest all that grass, bovines (as well as camels, giraffes, deer, antelopes, sheep, and goats) have a special ability called rumination, or chewing the cud. This special system of digestion allows them to eat a lot at one time, chew the food only briefly, swallow it almost whole to store it, and rechew it at leisure later on.

In the Wild

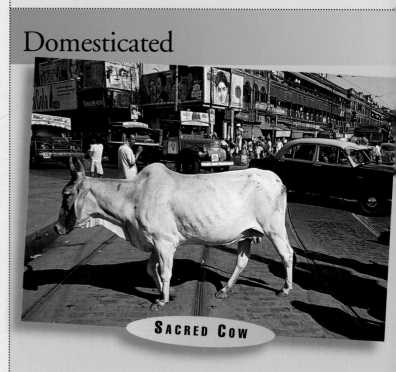

YAKS

The shaggy yaks of Asia live at higher altitudes than most mammals. Although a few still live in the wild, the yaks have also been **domesticated,** used for centuries by people of the Himalayas as a beast of burden and for its meat, milk, and wool.

Domesticated

SACRED COW

Zebus, a breed of Asian cattle, can be found wandering the streets of India like window-shoppers. They are considered sacred among people of the Hindu religion. Hindus will not eat them.

Chewing the Cud

Mammals that can chew their cud usually have four different stomach chambers (camels have three, humans have only one). First, vegetation is swallowed only partly chewed, going into chambers 1 and 2. There it is broken down by bacteria into pulp (called "cud") and sent back to be chewed again. After being rechewed, the cud is sent to chambers 3 and 4, where it is further broken down by **microorganisms** and passed into the intestine. The process takes about 24 hours.

CAPE BUFFALO

MUSK OXEN

An African Cape buffalo coats itself with mud as protection against the searing heat and bothersome insects. All buffalo are fond of wallowing in ponds and mudholes.

Confronted by an enemy, the musk oxen of Alaska and Canada "circle the wagons." They form a ring around their calves, with their horns pointed out, to ward off predators.

WATER BUFFALO

TEXAS LONGHORNS

The water buffalo of Asia is frequently seen pulling a plow for a farmer. Despite its long, dangerous horns, the water buffalo is easily tamed and valued for its strength and its milk.

Like the bison and the cowboy, the Texas longhorn is an emblem of the American Wild West. Longhorns were once abundant on the frontier before their numbers dwindled.

Sure-footed Goats

Goat

Sheep

Let's Compare

Domestic goats and sheep are easy to tell apart; the wild species look more similar. Goats have narrower, lighter bodies than sheep. Sometimes male goats have chin beards. Goats prefer steep cliffs, whereas sheep graze a little lower on the mountains.

A long with cattle, goats and sheep are probably the most important farm animals on earth. They were among the first animals to be domesticated in the late Stone Age. People all over the world still rely on goats and sheep for wool, meat, milk, cheese, and butter. In the wild, goats and sheep live like other bovids, gathering in herds and grazing. Although all grazers can upset the ecological balance if they eat too much vegetation in one area, goats are especially destructive. Their ravenous appetites and famous "iron" stomachs allow them to eat everything—even metal. In some dry countries, where domestic goats roam freely, they have severely damaged local plant life.

Wild goats and sheep have horns like other bovids, and can use them violently if need be. But rather than fight cougars and wolves, goats prefer to head for the hills.

Where in the World?

Mountain goats live in western North America.

MOROCCAN GOAT

Tree Climber

In places where there is little grass, as in Morocco, some goats combine their two main talents—climbing and eating. This young goat stands on the branches of a tree so that it can strip away the leaves.

Fast FACTS

Name Mountain goat
Number of Species 1
Family Bovidae
Order Artiodactyla
Shoulder Height 90-120 cm (3-4 ft.)
Weight at Maturity 46-140 kg (101-309 lbs.)
Distribution Western North America
Habitat Steep slopes and cliffs in high mountain regions; descends to lower elevations in the winter.
Food Grass, mosses, lichens, woody plants, and herbs
Social Structure Large groups may gather in winter, but usually in groups of 4 or fewer; adult males often seen alone
Gestation Period 6 months
No. of Young per Pregnancy 1-2, rarely 3
Weight at Birth 3.2 kg (7 lbs.)
Longevity 14-18 years
Conservation Status Some populations have declined due to excessive hunting.

Relatives

SHEEP

Male **bighorn sheep** are called rams for good reason. Jousts of head-butting go on all year long but become particularly fierce during mating season. Protected during battle by double-layered skulls, rams can butt repeatedly for hours at a time until the weaker one walks away.

Fancy Footwork

A mountain-goat's hoof *(above)* has a hard outer edge for digging toeholds and a tough inner pad for gaining traction on sheer rock.

What Is a Carnivore?

A carnivore is any animal that eats meat. All sorts of mammals—from cats and dogs to bears and wolves—are carnivores. Some of them eat meat every day, others only once in a while. No matter what their diet, all carnivores have sharp teeth and strong stomachs so they can chew and digest raw meat.

Before a carnivore can kill another animal, it has to catch it. So it must have sharp ears, a good nose, and keen eyes. Above all, it must be able to outsmart, outrun, and overpower the animal it is trying to track down.

Because carnivores live by preying on other animals, they are called **predators;** the creatures they hunt are called **prey.** Predators usually have eyes near the front of their heads. This lets them see their prey as they pounce forward on it. Prey animals such as rabbits or deer, by contrast, have eyes on the sides of their heads. This lets them watch out for carnivores and dash away in time.

Fabulous Features!

The Better to Bite You With!

Carnivores have special molars, called carnassials *(right)*, that are perfect for ripping and shredding meat. Other mammals—such as humans, rodents, horses, and cows—have wide, flat molars that grind food rather than tear it.

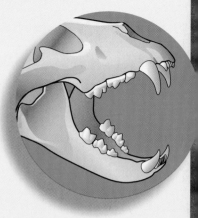

CARNASSIAL TEETH

Not Mean—Just Hungry!

Clutching a duck in her powerful jaws, a mother fox prepares to return to her den. Carnivores must kill other animals in order to survive and feed their young, so they hunt from instinct, not cruelty. Thanks to the success of this hunt, the fox and her kits will have a day-long feast.

Pretending to take a bite out of Dad is a lesson in real life for this lion cub. To survive as a carnivore, it must learn to attack and eat other animals.

Lions Kings of the Savanna

Lions often lounge around for 20 hours a day, just digesting their food. But when they get hungry, they become alert and deadly hunters. They stalk grass-eating animals—zebras, antelopes, and gazelles—that live in herds on the African savanna.

Like their prey, lions live in groups (they are the most social members of the cat family). A group, or pride, is led by one to three adult males. The rest of the pride consists of females and their cubs.

Each member of the pride has a clear-cut role. The females are responsible for hunting prey and raising cubs. The males protect the pride's territory—which may cover as much as 400 square km (155 sq. mi.)—by marking the boundaries with their claws and the scent of their urine. If that doesn't work, a male may drive off enemies, such as hyenas or rival males, in a fight.

Where in the World?

Most lions live in game preserves in East and South Africa.

Fast FACTS

Name Lion

Number of Species 1

Family Felidae

Order Carnivora

Head and Body Length 140-250 cm (4.6-8.2 ft.)

Weight at Maturity 120-250 kg (265-551 lbs.)

Distribution Protected areas of Africa and the Gir Forest in India

Habitat Semiarid regions, steppes, bush, wild savanna

Food Wildebeest, impala, other antelopes, giraffes, buffalo, wild hogs, and zebras, often carrion

Social Structure Pairs or prides of 30 or more

Gestation Period 3-4 months

No. of Young per Pregnancy 1-6, usually 3-4

Weight at Birth 1.3 kg (2.9 lbs.)

Longevity Average of 13 years in zoos, but some nearly 30 years

Conservation Status Threatened, except in protected areas

After You!

With a female and her cubs nearby, a male lion feasts on a zebra. Female lions hunt down and kill most prey, but the males often grab their share first. A male lion consumes as much as 30 kg (65 lbs.) of meat in a single meal.

Female Lions Are Masters of the Hunt.

Would **You** *Believe?*

Female lions run faster than males. With no big, dark mane, they are also better at sneaking up on prey. They practice co-operative hunting, in which two or more lionesses drive a prey animal toward a hidden pride.

Bitter Rivals

HYENAS

A pack of snarling hyenas corners a lioness. Although hyenas normally steer clear of healthy lions, they will not hesitate to at-tack a lion cub or an injured adult. Hyenas were once grouped in the dog family but are now recognized as a type of cat. They are natural enemies of lions because both compete for the same sources of food on the African savanna.

Cub Transporter

Not many creatures would feel secure in a lion's mouth, but this lion cub does. Its mother is moving the cub to a place where it will be safer from predators. Grabbing the cub by the scruff of its neck, the mother carries the young-ster without hurting it. (Did you notice those spots on the cub's fur? They will fade in time, but for now they help hide the cub from predators such as hyenas.)

Tigers Lone Hunters

The tiger is a large and lonely hunter. Not only is it the biggest member of the cat family, it is the most solitary: Except when a female is tending her cubs, most tigers prefer to live alone.

Tiger habitats range from the snowy forests of Siberia to the muggy jungles of Southeast Asia. These places allow the animal to hide as it stalks its prey, which includes deer, wild pig, wild ox, water buffalo, and the occasional slow monkey. If a tiger smells the scent marking another tiger's territory, it will turn away to avoid making contact with a rival hunter.

Tigers are **nocturnal**; they hunt mostly at night. They can see in dim light about six times better than humans. Why? Because tiger eyes have a dense layer of cells in their retinas that are sensitive to low light. These cells also reflect any light that shines on them, making the tiger's eyes appear to burn.

Camouflage is a natural pattern or color that helps an animal hide from its predators—or prey. The orange and black stripes of a tiger stand out in a zoo, but they allow the animal to blend into its native surroundings—trees and tall grasses (left).

How Big?

The Siberian tiger is the world's largest cat. It measures 2.75 to 3.5 m (9-12 ft.) long from head to tail, and about 1 m (3.5 ft.) tall at the shoulder. One male Siberian tiger weighed in at 385 kg (850 lbs.).

Where in the World?

Tiger habitats have dwindled to the areas shown in dark green in Asia.

White Tigers

A rare **mutation** that was highly valued by Indian royalty 100 years ago, white tigers were hunted for their rare coats. About 100 live in captivity today.

Would **You** **Believe?**

Fast FACTS

Name Tiger

Number of Species 1

Family Felidae

Order Carnivora

Head and Body Length 140-280 cm (4.5-9.2 ft.)

Weight at Maturity 65-306 kg (143-675 lbs.)

Distribution Pakistan, India, Siberia, Malay Peninsula, Sumatra

Habitat Tropical rain forests, evergreen forests, mangrove swamps, grasslands, and savannas

Food Large mammals (pigs, deer, antelope); occasionally smaller mammals and birds

Social Structure Solitary

Gestation Period 3 months

No. of Young per Pregnancy 1-6, usually 2-3

Weight at Birth .8-1.3 kg (1.7-3.5 lbs.)

Longevity 25 years at most

Conservation Status Endangered; some varieties nearly or totally extinct

Tyger! Tyger!
burning bright

In the forests of the night,
What immortal hand or eye
Could frame thy fearful symmetry?

William Blake (1757-1827)

Jaguars and Leopards

The jaguar *(right)* and the leopard *(opposite)* look and act somewhat alike, yet they live worlds apart. The jaguar's home is Central and South America; the leopard lives in Africa and Asia. Both animals have spotted coats, but the dot patterns differ. The jaguar has a thick body, massive jaws, and a short tail. The leopard's body is sleek and graceful; its jaws are narrow and its tail is long. Being lighter, the leopard also climbs trees more easily. They both have been hunted for their fur and are now endangered.

Fast FACTS

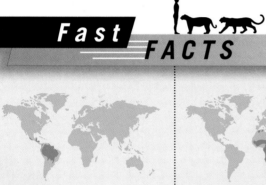

JAGUAR

Number of Species 1
Family Felidae
Order Carnivora
Head and Body Length 112-185 cm (3-6 ft.)
Weight at Maturity 36-158 kg (79-348 lbs.)
Distribution Mexico; Central and South America
Habitat Forests, savannas; in Mexico, scrub country and deserts
Food Large mammals (capybaras, tapirs, peccaries), crocodilians, fish, and domestic cattle
Social Structure Solitary
Gestation Period 3-3.5 months
No. of Young per Pregnancy 1-4, usually 2
Weight at Birth 900 g (2 lbs.)
Longevity Up to 22 years in captivity
Conservation Status Endangered

LEOPARD

Number of Species 1
Family Felidae
Order Carnivora
Head and Body Length 91-191 cm (3-6 ft.)
Weight at Maturity 28-90 kg (62-198 lbs.)
Distribution Africa; Middle East to southeastern Siberia, Asia
Habitat Lowland forests, mountains, grasslands, brush country, and deserts
Food Gazelles, wildebeests, wild pigs, deer, monkeys, and birds
Social Structure Solitary; sometimes in pairs or family groups
Gestation Period 3-3.5 months
No. of Young per Pregnancy 1-6, usually 2 or 3
Weight at Birth 500 g (1.3 lbs.)
Longevity 15-23 years
Conservation Status Endangered

JAGUAR

Jaguars live in equatorial rain forests, where they stalk or ambush all creatures great and small: capybaras, deer, peccaries (a type of wild pig), and tapirs, birds, and even mice. After killing its prey, a jaguar may drag the carcass to a secluded spot before eating it. In addition to being a powerful hunter, the jaguar is an excellent swimmer. It prefers to live near fresh water, where it can catch fish, turtles, and the small Latin American alligators known as caimans *(above)*.

A Jug from the Past

This jaguar-shaped drinking jug was made by a potter of the Moche culture in ancient Peru hundreds of years ago. The Moche, whose civilization flourished from the 3rd to the 8th century, revered the jaguar as the god of the night. They believed that the spots on its coat stood for the stars in the sky.

Step into My Larder!

Jaguar

Leopard

Jaguar and leopard spots both take the form of ring-shaped patterns called rosettes. But only the jaguar has one or more dark spots in the center of each ring.

LEOPARD

This leopard is tuckered out from a hard day's work. It has just killed a 45-kg (100-lb.) springbok and dragged its carcass up an acacia tree. The leopard stores its food this way to keep it safe from other predators. It will feed on the kill for the next several days. A leopard is so strong that it can climb a tree while hauling a carcass that weighs more than it does. It is such a good climber that it can come back down headfirst.

SNOW LEOPARD

Would You Believe?

A Black Panther?

The animal above, sometimes called a black panther, is in fact a leopard. It looks black from a distance; close up, however, faint spots can be seen on its dark coat. A single litter often includes both "black" and spotted leopard cubs.

Power, Grace, and Style

The rare snow leopard lives in the high mountains of the Himalayas. The champion jumper of all big cats, it can leap 15 m (50 ft.) in a single bound. This nimble climber on bare rock ranges as high as 6,000 m (20,000 ft.) in summer. In winter, it prowls forests below 1,800 m (6,000 ft.).

Cheetah Fastest Thing on Paws

The cheetah does not stalk its prey until it gets close enough to pounce on it. Instead, it streaks across the savanna at speeds up to 110 km/h (70 mph) and chases down the animal in the open. That style of hunting is just one of many traits that set the cheetah apart from other predatory cats. Its medium size, for example, puts it in a class of its own: Reaching about 70 kg (150 lbs.), the cheetah outweighs small cats such as the bobcat and lynx but cannot measure up to the big cats (lions, tigers, and jaguars). It is also diurnal, meaning it prefers to hunt by day.

The cheetah also stands out because its claws do. Whereas all other cats can pull in, or retract, their claws, the cheetah lives with its claws in the "out" position. As a result, the animal's claws are dull and less curved, making the cheetah poor at climbing trees; but the claws help with running.

Where in the World?

Cheetahs live in Africa and parts of the Middle East.

Peach Fuzz for Protection

A cheetah cub snuggles up to its mother. The long, fluffy fur will stay on its back until the cub is about 10 weeks old, making it look larger and more dangerous than it really is. Cheetah cubs remain with their mother for nearly 18 months, when they leave home in a pack of two to four cubs. To tell a cheetah from other cats, look for its polka-dot markings and a "teardrop" line running from each eye to the mouth.

Fast FACTS

Name Cheetah

Number of Species 1

Family Felidae

Order Carnivora

Head and Body Length 112-150 cm (3.5-5 ft.)

Weight at Maturity 35-72 kg (77-158 lbs.)

Distribution Africa, Asia

Habitat Semideserts, open grasslands, thick bush; avoids forests

Food Gazelles, impalas, other small to medium-sized ungulates; hares and other small mammals; birds

Social Structure Solitary or small groups

Gestation Period 3 months

No. of Young per Pregnancy 1-8, usually 3-5

Weight at Birth 150-300 g (5-11 oz.)

Longevity Up to 19 years in captivity

Conservation Status Vulnerable in Africa; endangered in Asia

A Spring-loaded Mammal

The cheetah is the world's fastest land animal because of its flexible backbone, which expands and contracts like a coiled spring as the cheetah runs. With its tail providing balance and its nonretractable claws gripping the ground like cleats, the cheetah can accelerate from 0 to 110 km/h (70 mph) in just three seconds. It's a wonder no one has named a car after it!

Helping Humans Hunt

Would **You** *Believe?*

Noblemen tamed cheetahs in ancient India and trained them to hunt. The captive cheetah would run after game (such as the antelope shown in the 16th-century painting at left), knock it down, then wait nearby for the master of the hunt to complete the kill. The pharaohs of Egypt also used cheetahs this way.

Small but Ferocious Cats

LYNX

The mammals on this page are smaller—and quieter!—than their relatives, the big cats. None of them—be it a cougar, a lynx, or a fishing cat—can roar. That's because the bones in their voice box are joined too tightly to make a roaring sound. Like their cousin the house cat, however, small cats can purr—and do so whenever they are especially content.

The lynx is unlike most other cats because the male helps care for his young. He brings food to the mother and her newborns until the kittens are about five months old. At that point the mother starts teaching them to hunt, and the father returns to his own territory.

Slightly smaller than the lynx is North America's most common wildcat, the bobcat. Its tail looks as if it has been "bobbed," or cut short. Bobcats live in swamps, grasslands, and deserts, but they hide so well that humans rarely see them.

Where in the World?

Only Australia and Antarctica have no small cats.

Catfish? No! Fishcat? Yes!

Most cats avoid water, but the fishing cat jumps in headfirst! Its water-resistant fur and partially webbed paws help this small wildcat catch fish.

FISHING CAT

Would You Believe?

Cat Mummy

No one knows who tamed the first cat, but cats were present in Palestinian towns 7,000 years ago. The ancient Egyptians, who kept cats as mouse hunters and pets 4,000 years ago, saw them as sacred. They mummified the bodies of cats that had died *(right)*.

Fast FACTS

Name Small cats

Number of Species 30

Family Felidae

Order Carnivora

Head and Body Length Smallest: black-footed cat, 34-50 cm (1-2 ft.); largest: cougar, 105-196 cm (3-6 ft.)

Weight at Maturity Black-footed cat, 1.5-2.8 kg (3.3-6 lbs.); cougar, 67-103 kg (148-227 lbs.)

Distribution All continents except Australia and Antarctica; absent from Arctic and oceanic islands

Habitat Varies, but majority live in forests or dry, open country

Food Mostly mammals and birds; also fish, amphibians, and reptiles

Social Structure Usually solitary

Gestation Period 2-3 months

No. of Young per Pregnancy 1-8

Weight at Birth 40-450 g (1-16 oz.)

Longevity Most to 15 years

Conservation Status Some species threatened or endangered

Chasing down dinner, a lynx pursues a snowshoe hare in Canada. Wide, thick paws help the lynx run across the snow without sinking into it.

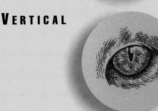

MEERKATS

Standing bolt upright on their hind legs, two meerkats guard the entrance to their underground den. Despite their name, meerkats are not cats; they belong to the mongoose family and are only distantly related to cats.

Let's Compare

CATS' PUPILS

The eyes of all cats but the cheetah have pupils that close to a vertical slit. This allows the pupil to open virtually all the way, letting maximum light into the eye at night. The cheetah, which hunts by day, has pupils that close to a circle. This keeps out bright sunlight and allows sharper focus and greater depth of field.

CIRCULAR

VERTICAL

A Cougar on the Prowl

The cougar—also known as the puma, the panther, and the mountain lion—is the largest American cat. A superb jumper, it has been known to leap 5.5 m (18 ft.) up into a tree. That's as high as a two-story house!

Pandas Cuddly Loners

Until the 1870s, few people knew about the giant panda. That's because this shy, almost secretive mammal lived a quiet life hidden away in the remote mountain forests of central China. In 1869 a French priest and naturalist named Armand David sent a panda skin and a description of the animal to the Museum of Natural History in Paris.

At the museum, the creature was dubbed a "giant panda" by **zoologists.** They thought it was related to the lesser panda—a much smaller reddish brown animal that also lives in Southeast Asia. Most modern zoologists think the giant panda belongs in the bear family and that the lesser panda is a member of the raccoon family, which is more distantly related to bears.

These mellow animals with their unusual coloring and banditlike mask are **endangered.** Only about 1,000 giant pandas still live in the wild.

Where in the World?

Pandas live in the mountains of central China.

Fast FACTS

Name Giant panda

Number of Species 1

Family Ursidae

Order Carnivora

Head and Body Length 120-150 cm (4-5 ft.)

Weight at Maturity 75-160 kg (165-353 lbs.)

Distribution Central China

Habitat Mountain forests

Food Almost exclusively bamboo shoots and roots; sometimes flower bulbs and tufted grasses

Social Structure Solitary, except during mating season

Gestation Period 3-5 months

No. of Young per Pregnancy 1 or 2, sometimes 3, but generally only a single cub survives

Weight at Birth 96-130 g (3-5 oz.)

Longevity 30 years in captivity

Conservation Status Endangered due to human encroachment on panda's habitat and poaching for their hides

Greens and Meat?

Pandas live almost entirely on bamboo, which would make them **herbivores,** but they are actually **omnivores;** the bones of small animals have been found in their stomachs. Their strong jaws and flat molars chew 35 kg (80 lbs.) of bamboo a day.

Bear Hugs

A mother panda gently carries her newborn cub *(right)* in her mouth. Pandas are born blind and with only skimpy white fur. Their birthweight may be as low as 90 g (3 oz.)—less than that of a mouse—which means their parents outweigh them 1,400 to 1 (no other **placental** mammal has a higher weight ratio of adults to young).

Living on a diet of mother's milk, the panda cub will grow a full coat of black-and-white fur by the end of its first month. By then, it will weigh nine times more than it did at birth. The cub will not open its eyes, however, until it is six to nine weeks old.

Relatives

The giant panda resembles the raccoon *(below)* because both have face masks and both handle food with their front paws. But the panda is like a bear, too, because the young are so tiny next to the adults. For these reasons, zoologists often argue about which family of animals—raccoons or bears—the panda fits into. Recent studies suggest that bears are in fact the panda's nearest relatives.

RACCOON

Fabulous Features!

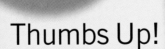

Thumbs Up!

If you've ever seen a video of a panda stripping leaves from a stem of bamboo, you might think the animal has a thumb. In a way, it does: Along with its five short fingers *(above),* the panda handles its food with a stubby bone—the sesamoid—that acts like a thumb. The sesamoid is called a "false thumb" because it grows from the panda's wrist, not its paw.

Conservation

A researcher transports a tranquilized panda at a wildlife center in China's Yellow Mountains to a safe place. Pandas, an endangered species, are protected by the Chinese government and international conservation organizations. Other nations must obtain a special permit to import the animals. But with panda pelts selling on the black market for as much as $10,000, the rare creatures are still occasionally targeted by poachers.

Habitat loss is an even bigger threat. From 1973 to 1984, half of the natural bamboo forests in China were cut down for farmland or timber.

Working together, the government of China and the World-Wide Fund for Nature are expanding panda reserves—and creating new ones.

Grizzly Bears

Fish...Eat...Sleep!

The grizzly bear is a brown bear, the world's largest land carnivore, which can stand 2.8 m (9 ft.) tall and weigh 780 kg (1,700 lbs.). Brown bears live around the world, but those living in the Rocky Mountains of North America have frosted white hair on their back, making them look grizzled.

In California, however, the grizzly appears only on the state flag. That's because ranchers in the state had hunted the bear to extinction by the 1920s (grizzlies sometimes kill and eat cattle). In all other states where it lives except Alaska, the grizzly is a threatened species.

Despite having the sharp canine teeth of a carnivore, a grizzly eats more plants than meat. It is therefore an **omnivore.** Munching on grass, berries, roots, and bulbs—plus the occasional salmon, elk, or moose—the grizzly stores up enough body fat to be able to nap through the entire winter.

Where in the World?

Brown bears live in Europe, Asia, and North America.

Fast FACTS

Name Brown bear

Number of Species 1

Family Ursidae

Order Carnivora

Head and Body Length 170-280 cm (5.5-9 ft.)

Weight at Maturity 70-780 kg (154-1,716 lbs.)

Distribution Europe, Asia, North America

Habitat Tundras, alpine meadows, mountains, forests, seashores, riverbanks

Food Grasses, roots, berries; salmon, insects; other mammals

Social Structure Solitary; large groups at food sources

Gestation Period 6-9 months

No. of Young per Pregnancy 1-4, usually 2

Weight at Birth 340-680 g (12-24 oz.)

Longevity 30 years in the wild

Conservation Status Some subspecies threatened, but survival of the species considered assured

Do Not Disturb!

A Bear in Winter

Bears spend most of the winter dozing in a den, but they don't hibernate like ground squirrels, marmots, and other animals whose body temperatures drop to near freezing. In late fall, the grizzly bear digs a den and lines it with branches or grass. It then crawls inside and nods off. Though its heart rate and breathing slow down, its body temperature drops only a few degrees—and the bear wakes up quickly if disturbed! During this time the pregnant female gives birth, then nurses the cubs in her sleep.

Open wide for salmon: A grizzly bear catches a leaping salmon in midair. The fish swim upstream to spawn, or lay eggs, in the spring, an easy food source.

BLACK BEAR

"Black" bears can be dark brown, reddish brown, or even white. Smaller and less heavy than a brown bear, the black bear is a good climber.

Would You Believe?

Walk This Way

Grizzly bears walk in each other's paw prints. That's why these tracks, from a centuries-old bear trail in Denali Park, Alaska, are so deep. Some bear trails cut 15 cm (6 in.) deep into solid ground.

The name "grizzly" may come from "grisly," meaning "causing a feeling of horror," or from the silver-tipped hairs on the bear's back, which give it a frosted or "grizzled" look.

Polar Bears Hunters on Ice

Not many plants grow in the northern lands where polar bears live, so the huge mammals must be crafty hunters to survive. They prey on fish and seabirds, and sometimes caribou, but ringed seals are the staple of their diet. In fact, a polar bear eats one seal about every 11 days, on average.

Because seals move so fast through water, the bear must figure out how to catch one near land. One tactic the bear uses is to stand very still beside a seal's breathing hole in the ice—sometimes for hours on end—until a seal pops its head up for air. The bear then strikes quickly, killing the seal with one swipe of its huge paw.

A polar bear may also wriggle forward on its belly toward a seal resting on the ice. Taking care to stay downwind, the polar bear grabs the seal before it can escape to the sea.

Like other bears, they sleep in a den during the worst part of the winter.

How Big?

A full-grown polar bear may tower 3.5 m (11 ft.) tall when it rears up on its hind legs *(right)*. That height comes in handy for spotting seals a long way off on flat ice. A typical male weighs about 450 kg (1,000 lbs.)—but some have reached more than 800 kg (1,750 lbs.)!

Where in the World?

Polar bears live along northern coasts.

Bear-ly Findable

What's the safest way to follow a polar bear? Use a satellite! If the bear has been fitted with a collar that sends radio signals to a satellite, researchers can track the animal from other continents.

Fast FACTS

Name Polar bear

Number of Species 1

Family Ursidae

Order Carnivora

Head and Body Length 200-250 cm (6-8 ft.)

Weight at Maturity 150-500 kg (330-1,100 lbs.)

Distribution Arctic

Habitat Arctic regions

Food Mainly seals and seabirds; also carcasses of marine mammals, reindeer, fish, vegetation

Social Structure Solitary or females with cubs; large groups near abundant food sources

Gestation Period 6.5-9 months

Number of Young per Pregnancy 1-4, usually 2

Weight at Birth 600 g (21 oz.)

Longevity 25-30 years

Conservation Status Vulnerable

Water World

Drip-dry from a Cool Dip

An excellent swimmer, the polar bear can swim across 65 km (40 mi.) of open water. A layer of fat 7.5 cm (3 in.) thick keeps the animal warm in near-freezing water. As soon as the polar bear leaves the water *(left)*, it shakes itself dry—or, as shown above, it rubs off the moisture on the snow and rolls around.

Fabulous **Features!**

Come Meet My Paw!

All bears have fur on their paws, but those of the polar bear are extra hairy *(above, right)*. The fur provides warmth and keeps the bear from slipping on ice. The large, broad front paws *(right)* are even more specialized: They are partly webbed, allowing the polar bear to swim for 40 km (25 mi.) or more at a stretch.

Still Hunting

Waiting for pups to pop up, three polar bears get ready to ambush their favorite prey— young seals. This behavior, in which a predator waits silent and unmoving for its victim to appear at a certain spot, is called still hunting. The tactic is not quite as random as it seems. Still hunting conserves energy. And a polar bear can smell a seal swimming beneath a layer of ice that is covered by 3 m (10 ft.) of snow.

Dog Family

Wolves on the Prowl

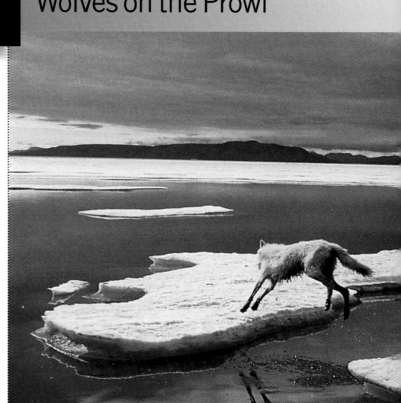

Wolves—the largest members of the dog family—don't deserve their bad reputation. True, they are fierce **predators** but they are also patient, generous, and cooperative— and they make excellent parents.

There are two species of wolf. The gray wolf, also called the timber wolf, lives mainly in central Asia, Siberia, and North America; a few live in remote areas of northern Europe and the Middle East. The second species, the red wolf, is far more rare and is only living in wildlife preserves in North Carolina and islands off the coasts of South Carolina and Mississippi.

Wolves live in family groups, called packs, of seven to 20 animals. Two leaders—the alpha male and alpha female—are responsible for the welfare of the entire pack. When pups are born, the mother tends them in her den; the father brings food.

Where in the World?

Wolves live in the areas shown here.

Cooperating to Kill

Three wolves team up to chase down a musk ox on Ellesmere Island in the Arctic. The wolves work together to isolate one animal from the herd, then drive it toward other wolves waiting in ambush. This behavior, called cooperative hunting, requires intelligence and teamwork, but it does not always work. Even after launching more than a dozen attacks in a row, a wolf pack may fail to bring down a strong or feisty prey animal.

Fast FACTS

Name Wolf

Number of Species 2

Family Canidae

Order Carnivora

Head and Body Length 100-160 cm (3.2-5.2 ft.)

Weight at Maturity 20-80 kg (44-176 lbs.)

Distribution Eurasia, Middle East, and North America

Habitat All Northern Hemisphere habitats except tropical forests and deserts

Food Gray wolf: large mammals (deer, bison); red wolf: small prey

Social Structure Family group with an adult pair and their offspring; hunt in packs

Gestation Period 2 months

No. of Young per Pregnancy 1-12, usually 4-7

Weight at Birth 450 g (1 lb.)

Longevity In wild, usually 4 years

Conservation Status Thriving in Alaska, Canada, and northern Asia; endangered in other areas

Arctic Wolves

An arctic wolf leaps from one ice floe to another as it searches its territory for food. Arctic wolves hunt caribou, musk oxen, lemmings, arctic hares, and even mice. A single wolf pack may roam a territory of 2,600 sq. km (1,000 sq. mi.).

Fabulous **Features!**

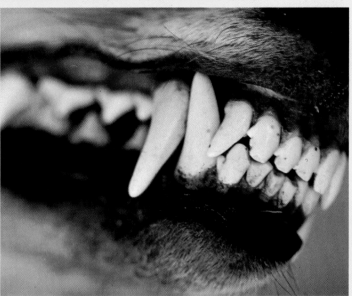

Teeth and Eyes

Like all carnivores, wolves have sharp, interlocking side teeth *(above)*. These fangs, called **canines,** are deadly weapons designed to grip prey and pierce flesh. Like domestic dogs, wolf pups are born with blue eyes; after a few months, however, their eyes turn yellow *(left)*.

Howl Are You?

A wolf howl sounds spooky to human ears, but it's just the way these animals communicate. Wolves howl when they're happy or lonely. They howl to call the pack together, or to warn other wolves away. Once one starts up, the rest often join in *(below)*.

"My, What Big Teeth You Have!"

Once upon a time, when wolves were common in Europe, parents kept children away from the woods by telling scary stories like "Little Red Riding Hood" *(left)*. They needn't have bothered: Gray wolves, shy of people, don't attack.

Dog Family Close up

Featured on these pages are some of the wolf's relatives in the extended dog family, the Canidae. (Pet dogs are members, too.)

The animals differ in shape, size, and temperament, but all of them have deep-chested bodies, a bushy tail, and erect ears. Unlike bears, who are among their closest relatives, dogs walk on their toes; this lets them run fast. And unlike cats, whose sharp, retractable claws are used for seizing prey, members of the dog family use their thick, nonretractable claws to dig dens.

Thanks to their superior endurance, dogs overcome their prey by running it down. It helps that they are social animals, meaning they live and hunt as a group. This allows these carnivores to catch larger animals than they could if they hunted alone; the bigger prey, in turn, is ample to feed a large group of predators. Many dogs mate for life, and all members of a dog family help feed and care for the young ones.

LOONEY TUNES, CHARACTERS, NAMES AND ALL RELATED INDICIA ARE TRADEMARKS OF WARNER BROS. INC. ©1997

HUNTING DOG

African hunting dogs *(above)* prey on zebras, impalas, and wildebeests. The mottled pattern of each dog's fur is unique.

COYOTE

Unlike its cartoon cousin, Wile E. Coyote *(top)*, a real-life coyote—seen pouncing on a field mouse, above—is an able hunter.

RED FOX

Four red fox kits wait for their mother to return to the den. In a few weeks they will follow along on the hunt.

A pack of jackals fight over a choice piece of an animal carcass. The animals belong to one of the four jackal species that live on the savanna, or grassy plain, of southern and eastern Africa. (One species, the golden jackal, is also found in southeast Europe and southern Asia.) Because jackals eat the same sorts of food that lions do, they often let the larger predators do their killing for them. Then, once the lions have finished feeding on the carcass, the jackals jump in and polish off the leftovers.

From Tame to Wild

Two dingoes—wild dogs that live in Australia—snap and snarl at each other as they fight for the right to be "top dog"—that is, leader of their pack. Dingoes are feral, meaning they were once tamed by humans but have now returned to the wild state. Stone Age hunters from Asia—ancestors of the modern-day Australian Aborigines—brought their pet dogs with them when they rowed canoes across the Indian Ocean to reach Australia. Once the dogs arrived on the island continent, however, they reverted, or turned back, into the wild dogs now known as dingoes.

DINGOES

From Wild to Tame

DOMESTIC DOG

A team of Siberian huskies work together to pull a sled over the snow of Alaska. Of all domestic dogs, the husky bears the strongest resemblance to the wolf. Indeed, with its narrow muzzle, pointed ears, thick fur, and long legs, the husky is often mistaken for a wolf from a distance. Like its wild relative, a Siberian husky is usually devoted to its pack leader—in this case, its human owner. Recent studies show that domestic dogs are direct descendants of wolves and may have been tamed by humans as long as 100,000 years ago. That is far older than house cats who probably were not tamed until 7,000 years ago.

Skunks and Smelly Relatives

Skunks stink—but only when they are in danger, and only as a last resort.

Skunks belong to the mustelid family, which includes weasels, otters, and all the animals shown here. They occupy every type of habitat. All members of this family are known for their bad odor, but the skunk is feared the most. A skunk gives an enemy plenty of notice before it sprays its putrid stench. First, it stamps its front paws on the ground. If that doesn't work, the skunk lifts its tail in warning. (One species, the spotted skunk, even stands on its front paws when threatening.) If the enemy still lurks, the skunk squirts an oily, noxious liquid from musk glands under its tail. The liquid, which can travel 4.5 m (15 ft.), briefly chokes and blinds the skunk's victim and stinks to high heaven!

Most animals learn to avoid skunks after their first run-in with one.

Where in the World?

Mustelids are found worldwide, but skunks live only in the New World.

Fast FACTS

Name Mustelids

Number of Species 65

Family Mustelidae

Order Carnivora

Head and Body Length Smallest: least weasel, 11.4 cm (4.5 in.); largest: wolverine, 1 m (3 ft.)

Weight at Maturity Least weasel, 25-250 g (.88-9 oz.); wolverine, 7-32 kg (15-71 lbs.)

Distribution All continents except Australia and Antarctica

Habitat Varies from open tundra to deep forest, from desert to fresh and salt water

Food Other mammals, birds, reptiles, fish, and small invertebrates

Social Structure Usually solitary, except during breeding season

Gestation Period 1-2 months

No. of Young per Pregnancy 1-18, usually 3-6

Weight at Birth 3-100 g (.1-3.5 oz.)

Longevity 5-20 years in the wild

Conservation Status Species hunted or trapped for their fur now are rare or endangered

Super Digger

The American badger *(right)*, a close relative of the skunk, spends most of its life underground chasing mice and insects. Its curved claws are so strong that it can tunnel through the dirt fast enough to catch a prairie dog!

BADGER

Color Changer

ERMINE

An ermine is poised to catch a frog for dinner, though its main diet consists of rodents. Over eons, it has adapted to its environment: From spring to fall, its brown coat helps it hide in the woods. In winter, its fur turns white to blend in with the snow.

Fierce Fighter

WOLVERINE

Ferocious for its size—about 27 kg (60 lbs.) full-grown—the wolverine attacks almost any animal that tries to interfere with it. A wolverine can catch and kill a sick moose or elk.

Would **You** *Believe?*

Pépé Le Pet

With its scent glands surgically removed, a skunk can make a cuddly pet.

Otters At Home in the Water

Doing back floats in the ocean, playful sea otters seem far removed from skunks. Yet they both belong to the mustelid family *(pages 66-67)*. Although otters spend most of their time in the water, they have the same sort of external ears, forepaws, and well-developed hind legs that land mammals do. They are also well-equipped for their water world, with webbed feet and a long tail that acts as a rudder.

A thick, furry coat protects the otter from the frigid waters of the northern Pacific. The animals constantly groom these coats by licking them; this keeps dirt out and ensures that an insulating layer of air bubbles stays trapped in the fur.

In the 19th century, sea otters were hunted for their luxurious furs. The furs were so highly prized that sea otters became nearly extinct. International treaties now ban hunting, and otters are slowly recovering.

Where in the World?

Sea otters live on the coasts and islands of the northern Pacific Ocean.

A wild otter *(left)* accepts a squid from human hands—a sure sign that otters are tame by nature. Their friendliness, sadly, once made them easy targets for fur traders. The California sea otter was thought to be extinct until 1938, when a rancher spotted a group of them near Big Sur. "Had you reported dinosaurs," said one scientist, "we couldn't have been more utterly dumbfounded."

She Saves Sea Otters by the Seashore

One person can make a difference: Margaret Owings founded Friends of the Sea Otter in 1968—the year she found otters lying on the beach shot by abalone fishermen who fear the otters' competition for abalone. Owings's group defeated a bill that would have legalized shooting sea otters in California. This is one reason otters are slowly coming back.

Fast FACTS

Name Sea otter

Number of Species 1

Family Mustelidae

Order Carnivora

Head and Body Length 100-120 cm (3.2-3.9 ft.)

Weight at Maturity 15-45 kg (33-99 lbs.)

Distribution Coasts and islands of the northern Pacific Ocean

Habitat Coastal waters, rarely more than 1 km (.62 mi.) from shore

Food Slow-moving fish and marine invertebrates

Social Structure Solitary while feeding; sometimes rests in concentrations of up to 2,000

Gestation Period 6.5-9 months

No. of Young per Pregnancy 1, rarely 2

Weight at Birth 1.4-2.3 kg (3-5 lbs.)

Longevity Up to 23 years

Conservation Status Hunted almost to extinction but now protected; populations recovering

Survival Skills

Diving for Dinner

Sea otters spend much of their day diving along rocky seashores for their favorite foods: abalones, clams, mussels and other mollusks, sea urchins, and crabs. Because they are so active, sea otters must consume 25 percent of their body weight in food each day. In devising ways to eat shellfish, they have shown an ingenuity that ranks them with chimpanzees and humans as tool users.

A sea otter will plunge underwater, grab a sea urchin or mollusk with one forepaw and a rock with the other, then return to the surface. Lying on its back with the stone on its stomach, the otter bangs the shellfish on the rock until it gets to the tasty meat inside *(left)*.

Vanishing quickly from sight, two river otters dive for fish. Of the 13 otter species, only one is a true sea otter. Like the sea otter, river otters have thick fur coats and webbed feet, making them more at home in the water than on land.

Adopting a favorite pose— floating on its back in the sea—an otter prepares to break open a spiny sea urchin with a rock.

What Is a Rodent?

CAPYBARA

Rodents—the world's largest order of mammals—are animals whose teeth never rest. A rodent has two long incisors—front teeth ideal for cutting—on its upper jaw and two more on its lower jaw. Because these incisors never stop growing, the animal must constantly wear them down. Gnawing does just that. It also sharpens them to a beveled edge, like that of a chisel.

Mice, rats, voles, squirrels, and beavers are just five of the 1,814 rodent **species** that live in environments from the tropics to the Arctic regions. Some, such as squirrels, specialize in climbing. Others run, swim, jump, burrow, or—in the case of "flying" squirrels—glide. The smallest rodent—and one of the smallest mammals—is the pygmy jerboa. It measures just 4 cm (1.6 in.) from head to tail. The largest rodent, the capybara, is 1.2 m (4 ft.) long.

Where in the World?

Rodents live all over the globe.

RED SQUIRREL

A red squirrel nibbles on a nut. Acorns and hickory nuts are its chief sources of nutrition. To protect its territory, a red squirrel will scold intruders or chase them away. It makes a nest of leaves in the treetops, where it raises two sets of triplets a year.

Fast FACTS

Name Rodents

Number of Species 1,814

Family 29 families

Order Rodentia

Head and Body Length Smallest: pygmy jerboa, 4-5 cm (1.5-2 in.); largest: capybara, 100-130 cm (3.3-4 ft.)

Weight at Maturity Pygmy jerboa: 2.5-12 g (.09-.42 oz.); capybara: 27-79 kg (60-174 lbs.)

Distribution Nearly worldwide

Habitat Varies from Arctic tundra to temperate and tropical forests, savannas, and deserts

Food Grain, fruits, nuts, invertebrates, and small vertebrates

Social Structure Some are solitary or in pairs, others live in colonies

Gestation Period 19 days-3 months

No. of Young per Pregnancy 2-12

Weight at Birth 1-1,500 g (.03 oz.- 3 lbs.)

Longevity 2-6 years in the wild

Conservation Status Mostly abundant and widespread

MUSKRAT

A muskrat busily builds its shelter in a riverbank *(above)*. Found throughout Canada and the United States, the muskrat has a flattened tail that helps it steer underwater. Muskrats are semiaquatic; that means they live near water and spend a lot of time in it. The name "muskrat" comes from the powerful, musky smell the rodent creates by its gland secretions.

Surrounded by caimans, a capybara—the world's largest rodent—basks on a riverbank in Brazil. The caimans will not attack the capybara unless it goes in the water, where they can move more quickly.

Fabulous **Features!**

A Gnawing Concern

Yellow is a sign of healthy teeth in rodents like the gray squirrel shown above. It comes from **keratin**—a hard enamel coating that protects against decay. The woodchuck above had misaligned jaws; unable to wear the incisors down, they grew so long that the animal could not eat.

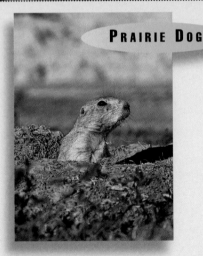

PRAIRIE DOG

Prairie dogs are not dogs, but they do make a high-pitched bark. Highly social animals, they dig long tunnels, or burrows, that connect underground, forming a prairie-dog "village."

True Hibernation

To avoid cold weather and a scarce food supply in winter, the ground squirrel *(below)* hibernates. Its heart and breathing slow, and its body temperature drops to near freezing to conserve energy and water.

GROUND SQUIRREL

Beavers Those Dam-Builders

Beavers, North America's largest rodents, change the environment. They cut down large and small trees by gnawing through the trunks. Together with smaller branches, these trunks form the framework of a dam across a stream, which in turn slowly creates a pond for the beaver to live in.

Once the dam is complete, the beaver tackles a second major construction project: It builds its home, called a **lodge,** in the middle of the pond, which makes it safe from most **predators.** The beaver returns to its dam every day to repair any leaks; it may even cut a spillway so water can escape when the water level gets too high.

The fashion rage for coats and tall hats made of beaver fur nearly wiped out the animals by the end of the 18th century. But when the clothes went out of style, their original owners—the beavers—began to rise in number again.

Where in the World?

Beavers live in North America and Eurasia.

Hard Teeth for Hard Work

A beaver's **incisors** are coated with a hard enamel. They are also beveled (slanted on one side), so the beaver uses them like a wood chisel. Working in shifts, two beavers can gnaw through an aspen tree 25 cm (10 in.) in diameter in less than four hours.

Beaver Paddles

A beaver has webbed hind feet. These powerful paddles push the animal through the water at 8 km/h (5 mph).

Home Wet Home!

A beaver lodge (*below*) has a built-in security system. To keep predators away from their kits, as young beavers are called, the adults build the entry tunnel underwater. Any intruder would first have to find this hidden opening—and be able to swim through it—to reach the nest chamber.

Fast FACTS

Name Beaver

Number of Species 2

Family Castoridae

Order Rodentia

Head and Body Length 60-80 cm (2-2.6 ft.)

Weight at Maturity 12-25 kg (26-55 lbs.)

Distribution North America, north and central Europe, northern Asia

Habitat Streams and small lakes

Food Bark, twigs, leaves, and roots of deciduous trees and shrubs; parts of aquatic plants

Social Structure Family or colony consisting of a mated pair of adults and the young of 2 years

Gestation Period 3.2-3.5 months

No. of Young per Pregnancy 1-9, usually 2-4

Weight at Birth 230-630 g (.5-1.4 lbs.)

Longevity 35-50 years in captivity

Conservation Status Thriving in North America, northern Europe

The Sign of the Beaver

PORCUPINE

Armed with new building materials—two tree branches—a beaver heads for home *(above)*. A beaver's presence is easy to spot by the felled and gnawed-on trees near a stream *(right)*. In addition to erecting their own houses, beavers turn streams into ponds and forests into wetlands.

Beavers also eat the bark, twigs, and roots of birch and willow trees. In the fall, a beaver may stick branches into the bottom of the pond, where the food stays fresh and handy all winter.

Only a cartoon porcupine can shoot its quills. In real life, the porcupine—a cousin of the beaver—swats an attacker with its spiny tail, lodging barbed quills into the victim's skin. Native Americans use dyed porcupine quills to decorate clothing as well as household objects like this box.

A beaver slices sleekly through the water. The animal's tail, about 40 cm (16 in.) long, is used for steering; its webbed hind feet supply the power. Closing its nostrils and holding its breath, the beaver can stay underwater for 15 minutes.

Rabbits and Hares

I'm All Ears!

Rabbits and their larger cousins, the hares, are built for survival. They have no weapons to fend off enemies, so they must be alert—and run fast!—to stay alive.

Rabbits' eyes bulge from each side of their head. They help the rabbit see ahead, behind, above, and to the sides without turning its head—a possibly fatal move, since it might draw the notice of a **predator.** Jack rabbits—hares so named because their large ears resemble those of a jackass—can turn their ears in opposite directions, enabling them to pick up any sound. If the jack rabbit has to flee, it can do so at 50 km/h (30 mph).

Rabbits also survive by sheer numbers. A couple can raise 30 babies a year. If all those lived, and each one had 30 babies of its own, there would be 24,300,000 rabbits in the family after five years. But predators and disease keep populations in check.

Sensing danger nearby, a jack rabbit freezes in place. This tactic may fool some predators, such as hawks and buzzards, which hunt visually and give up if the prey is not moving.

Where in the World?

Rabbits and hares are found nearly the world over.

Fast FACTS

Name Rabbit and hare

Number of Species 47

Family Leporidae

Order Lagomorpha

Head and Body Length 21.5-70 cm (8.5-27.5 in.)

Weight at Maturity .25-7 kg (.5-15 lbs.)

Distribution Worldwide

Habitat Forests, shrub-overgrown areas, grasslands, tundra, alpine slopes

Food Herbaceous vegetation: in winter may also eat buds, bark, and twigs

Social Structure Rabbits live in groups; most hares are solitary

Gestation Period 25-50 days

No. of Young per Pregnancy 2-8

Weight at Birth 35-50 g (1.2-1.8 oz.)

Longevity 1-5 years in the wild; 9 or more years in captivity

Conservation Status Some species rare; others so prevalent they are considered pests

Take That!

Have you ever heard the expression "mad as a March hare"? It comes from the way male rabbits and hares act in early spring. At the start of mating season, they fight each other like boxers (*above*) to prove which male is stronger.

Is Any Bunny Home?

European rabbits live in warrens—complex networks of interconnected tunnels. Hares do not dig; instead, they live in nests on the ground where the grass is tall enough to hide them from sight.

Let's Compare

Rabbit

Hare

How can you tell a rabbit from a hare? As shown above, rabbits have shorter ears than hares. Rabbits have shorter legs, too, so they cannot swing their hind legs ahead of their front legs when they run (hares can).

Sloths Just Hanging Out

Fabulous Features!

Some people say that sloths live up to their name, which means laziness. After all, these South American mammals spend a week or more hanging upside down in the same tree. They only descend to the ground once a week to relieve themselves. Sloths are nocturnal, meaning they sleep all day and feed at night. Even then, they move very slowly, hand over hand, along branches in the rain forest.

Sloths are built for a topsy-turvy existence. Their long, powerful arms end in strong claws or toes. Some have two toes, others have three. Their fur grows backward, not from their backs to their bellies but from their bellies to their backs, so that the rain will drain off easily. They can also turn their heads almost completely around. With these odd bodies, sloths manage to eat, sleep, raise their babies, and hide from jaguars—without ever moving too fast.

Where in the World?

Sloths live in Central and South America.

Arm Power

A sloth's arms end not in fingers but in sharp, 10-cm-long (4-in.-long) claws that hook over branches. Their forearms are longer than their upper arms and so flexible they barely have to move to pull leaves from trees. Their hind legs are short.

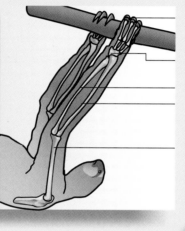

- Claws
- Wrist Bones
- Forearm (Ulna)
- Forearm (Radius)
- Upper Arm (Humerus)

Hair of a Young Adult Sloth

Green Hair?

Sloths have thick, gray-brown hair. Each hair has tiny cracks that get bigger as the sloth ages, as shown enlarged at right. During the rainy season, green algae (tiny plants) grow in these cracks, until the whole animal looks like it has green fur, and it is well hidden among the green leaves.

Hair of an Old Sloth

Fast FACTS

Name Three-toed sloth

Number of Species 3

Family Bradypodidae

Order Xenarthra

Head and Body Length 41-70 cm (1.3-2.3 ft.)

Weight at Maturity 2.3-5.5 kg (5-12 lbs.)

Distribution Central and South America

Habitat Arboreal in rain forest trees

Food Young leaves, tender twigs, and buds

Social Structure Solitary

Gestation Period 5-6 months

No. of Young per Pregnancy 1

Weight at Birth 200-250 g (7-9 oz.)

Longevity Not reported, but probably at least 20-30 years

Conservation Status All species jeopardized by lumbering and habitat destruction; one species in coastal forest in Brazil is endangered

Hidden in the Canopy
of the Rain Forest

Emergent Layer

Canopy

Understory

Forest Floor

Love Those Buds

Sloths in the wild live almost entirely on leaves, buds, and young twigs. Clinging to a branch high in the canopy of the rain forest, they pull the leaves slowly toward them with their claws. Then they grind up their dinners with big teeth in their cheeks. To digest this tough food, they have several chambers in their stomachs, like cattle or sheep.

How **Slow** Do Sloths Go?

Sloths are the slowest mammals on earth. At its fastest, a sloth travels 1.5 m (5 ft.) per minute. On the ground, it can't stand upright, but will drag itself along with its claws.

Anteaters

When an anteater is on the prowl, no ant—or termite—is safe. Although ants burrow underground, and termites build rock-hard mounds for protection, the anteater has two powerful weapons. One is its pair of heavy front claws. The other is its long, sticky tongue. With these tools the anteater can rip open any anthill or termite mound and feast on the scurrying insects inside.

Anteaters live in the forests and grassy plains of Central and South America. The four species of these mammals range in size from the tree-dwelling silky anteater, 38 cm (15 in.) long, to the ground-based giant anteater, 1.8 m (6 ft.) long including its tail. None of them has teeth, but anteaters do have long, skinny, muscular tongues covered with sticky saliva. After an anteater has torn into a termite mound, it flicks its tongue into the heap and pulls it out covered with insects. It then contentedly chews up the termites using—instead of teeth—small bony knobs inside its mouth.

Anteaters would rather run than fight. When threatened, the giant anteater will move off in a slow, shuffling gallop. But if anteaters are cornered, watch out: Those big claws can be a slashing defense.

Where in the World?

Anteaters roam Latin America; pangolins live in Africa and Asia.

Fast FACTS

Name Giant anteater

Number of Species 1

Family Myrmecophagidae

Order Xenarthra

Head and Body Length 100-120 cm (3.3-4 ft.)

Weight at Maturity 18-39 kg (39-86 lbs.)

Distribution Tropical and subtropical Central and South America

Habitat Savannas, grasslands, swampy areas, humid forests

Food Ants, termites, beetle larvae

Social Structure Solitary

Gestation Period 5-6 months

No. of Young per Pregnancy 1

Weight at Birth 1-2 kg (2.2-4.4 lbs.)

Longevity Nearly 26 years in captivity

Conservation status Vulnerable due to habitat loss and expansion of human population in Central America and hunting in South America

Fabulous Features!

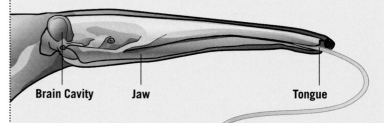

Brain Cavity　　**Jaw**　　**Tongue**

Hose Nose

The giant anteater's skull is almost all toothless jaw, with a mouth no wider than a pencil. The bones of the skull are hard and thick. The tongue, attached to muscles way back in the animal's rib cage, can extend 58 cm (23 in.) out of its mouth.

Dig This

All anteaters have big, sharp claws on their front feet. On the giant anteater, these are 10 cm (4 in.) long. The claws let the animals pull apart anthills and termite mounds. They are also effective weapons in the animal's defense. But the curved claws make walking awkward. To avoid stepping on their claws, giant anteaters walk on their knuckles. Collared anteaters walk on the outside of their hands.

Relatives

ARMADILLO

SILKY ANTEATER

The armadillo is a different-shaped ant and insect eater covered with horny plates. When scared, it curls up into an armored ball *(right)*.

The silky anteater will cover its face with its claws when in danger. This soft little creature lives mostly in trees, climbs with the use of a prehensile tail, and eats at night.

The Pangolin

The scale-covered pangolins, which live in Africa and Southeast Asia, look and act like anteaters and armadillos, but they belong to a separate order, the Pholidota. Their back, sides, and prehensile tail are covered with overlapping, horny scales. When threatened, the pangolin rolls itself up into a ball to protect its underside. The Asian species are endangered because their scales are often used in Chinese medicines. The species is now protected worldwide.

Would **You** *Believe?*

Anteaters can eat 30,000 termites a day! Their floppy, sticky tongues probe deep into termite mounds. Then they come out covered with termites and grubs for the anteater to munch.

Moles
Hedgehogs, Shrews
The Insect Eaters

SHREW

Insectivores—a group that includes moles, shrews, and hedgehogs—are small mammals, but big eaters. The name insectivore means "insect eater," but they chow down on a variety of meals, including worms, mice, birds, and even plants. They need to take in a lot of fuel to keep themselves going. Even tiny shrews must eat twice their own weight in food every day.

Insect eaters come in many shapes and sizes, but they usually have long, twitchy noses, little, pointed teeth, and tiny eyes and ears. The smallest of them—Savi's pygmy shrew—may be the smallest mammal on earth. Adults are only 4 cm (1½ in.) long and weigh 2 g (.07 oz.)—less than a dime.

Insectivores live all over the world, although you might not see them often. Moles burrow underground, and all other insect eaters tend to be solitary, nocturnal creatures who run and hide from people.

Shrews are the most common kind of insectivore. These tiny, sharp-nosed creatures are so nervous that they can literally die of fright at a loud noise. When skittish little baby shrews feel scared, they form a "caravan." One baby grabs the mother's fur in its mouth, the second grabs the first one, and so on, until the mother pulls them to safety.

Where in the World?

Moles live in Europe, northern Asia, and North America.

HEDGEHOG

Hedgehogs are known for the sharp spines that protect them. They have a strong muscle that runs along each side. When threatened, they pull in on this muscle and curl up into a thorny ball. If they squeeze between rocks or in a burrow, the spines make it impossible for a predator to dislodge them.

Fast FACTS

Name Mole

Number of Species 32

Family Talpidae

Order Insectivora

Head and Body Length 6.3-22 cm (2.4-8.6 in.)

Weight at Maturity 9-170 g (.3-6 oz.)

Distribution Europe, Asia, North America

Habitat Underground in meadows, clearings, and deciduous forests; some species are aquatic

Food Mainly worms and other small invertebrates; aquatic moles: insects, crustaceans, mollusks, fish

Social Structure Mostly solitary

Gestation Period 1-1.5 months

No. of Young per Pregnancy 1-7, usually 3-4

Weight at Birth 1-4 g (.03-.14 oz.)

Longevity About 4 years

Conservation Status Generally common; some species are trapped for fur and may be threatened

The Star-nosed Mole

Living in the dark, moles rely on their delicate snouts to find their way and sense food. The star-nosed mole has taken this to an extreme. Around its nose are 22 soft, pink "rays." The rays wiggle around as the mole looks for a meal underground in damp soil and underwater.

The Mole's Holes

Every mole digs an underground home and patrols its tunnels regularly. It carves out rooms for drinking water and a "bathroom" for waste disposal. Another room holds a supply of food. Female moles also build a central nest chamber where they rear their babies. If a male meets another male in a tunnel, they fight.

Mole at Work

"So he scraped and scratched and scrabbled and scrooged, and then he scrooged again and scrabbled and scratched and scraped, working busily with his little paws and muttering to himself, "Up we go! Up we go!" till at last, pop! his snout came out into the sunlight."

From The Wind in the Willows *by Kenneth Grahame*

The mole's short forearms with strong claws are turned outward for digging power. Its tiny eyes can barely see.

Bats Lords of Darkness

A swift shadow in the darkness, a tumbling, twirling acrobat of the air, the bat is a master of flight. In fact, bats are the only mammals that fly. The name of their order—Chiroptera—means "hand-wings." That's because a bat's wing is a hand whose stretched-out fingers are joined by leathery skin. Bats fly with a sculling motion, like a swimmer doing the butterfly stroke. Soaring as high as 3,000 m (10,000 ft.), they can reach speeds of 100 km/h (60 mph) with a good tailwind.

There are 986 species of bats. They live almost everywhere in the world, even on faraway islands in the Pacific. Some eat fruit and others feast on fish or frogs; some even drink animal blood, but most dine on insects. People should be grateful—without bats, there would be billions more harmful insects swarming in the air.

Where in the World?

Bats are found in every region of the world except Antarctica and the Arctic.

Fast FACTS

Name Bat

Number of Species 986

Family 18 families

Order Chiroptera

Head and Body Length Smallest: hog-nosed bat, 2.9-3.3 cm (1-1.3 in.); largest: flying fox, 17-41 cm (6.7-16 in.)

Weight at Maturity 2 g-1.5 kg (.07 oz.-3.3 lbs.)

Distribution Every continent except Antarctica and the Arctic regions

Habitat Wooded and brushy regions, often near caves and water

Food Most eat insects or fruit; others take nectar, pollen, small fish, frogs, reptiles, birds, mammals, or blood

Social Structure Colonies

Gestation Period 1.5-4.8 months

No. of Young per Pregnancy Mostly 1, some species bear 2

Weight at Birth Highly variable

Longevity 15-30 years

Conservation Status Some endangered, but most are abundant

How Bats Find Their Prey

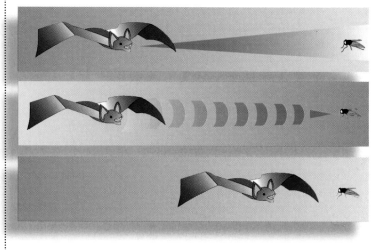

A hunting bat sends out ultrahigh-pitched squeaks through its mouth or nose. The sound bounces off an insect, and the echo returns to the bat, telling it where to find its prey.

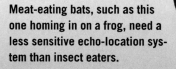

Meat-eating bats, such as this one homing in on a frog, need a less sensitive echo-location system than insect eaters.

The Bat's Crowded Cave

Bats roost hanging upside-down in large colonies . Some caves hold millions of the animals, packed in at 300 in a space of 75 square cm (1 sq. ft.). In the evening, they all fly out to hunt. When winter comes, the bats go into a deep sleep in their roost. If they are disturbed, they could die.

The Bat's Wing

A bat's wing looks like a hand with four long, skinny fingers and a small thumb.

Sweet Tooth

Flying foxes and other large fruit-eating bats live in Africa and southern Asia, finding their dinners by sight and a keen sense of smell. They are the largest bats in the world, and often have sweet, doglike faces. By dropping seeds on the ground as they eat, fruit bats help spread new fruit trees.

"**F**lower bats" and "bat flowers" seem to have a close friendship. Long-tongued bats carry pollen from flower to flower as they drink nectar, helping the flowers to reproduce. In turn, the flowers bloom at night, when the bats are flying. They have large blossoms so the bats can easily land and feed.

Vampire Bats

Out for Blood

Vampire bats scare people. After all, they drink blood. They have weird pushed-in noses and sharp front teeth. And in stories they are connected to frightening human vampires.

But there is little reason for people to fear vampire bats. These bats live only in Central and South America. Roosting in dark caves or old tunnels and wells, they fly out at night, low above the ground, looking for mammals or birds to prey on. They do drink blood, but they greatly prefer the blood of cows, pigs, and chickens. Their bite is really painless; when they chomp on a sleeping cow, for example, it does not even wake up. The bat does not lap up enough blood to hurt the animal—at most a bat drinks 20 ml (.7 fl. oz.) of blood per night, no more than four teaspoonfuls. Most important, the old stories of human vampires are not true. They are just good scary tales.

The Hopping Bat

Most bats launch themselves into flight from the roof of a cave or a tree. Vampire bats can take off from the ground. They take several steps to get airborne.

1 To start with, the bat hops around on feet and thumbs.

2 A push with a thumb will get things going.
3 Back on all fours, the bat gets ready for a big leap.
4 When it is at least 15 cm (6 in.) in the air, the bat spreads its wings and flies.

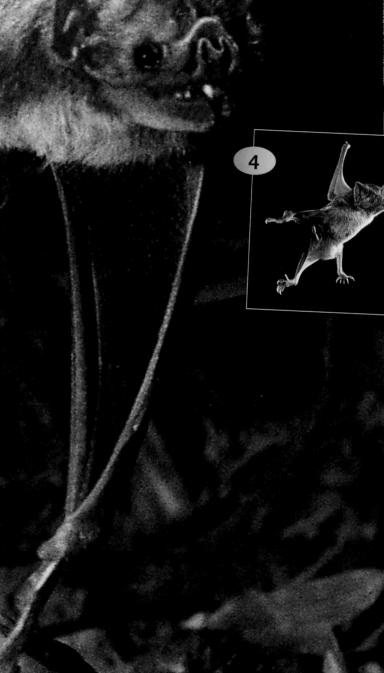

4

Some people say that vampire bats suck blood, but they don't—they lap it up. When the bat lands on a victim, usually a cow, horse, pig, or chicken, it first licks the skin. Then it bites with its big front teeth, leaving a small, shallow, bleeding wound. Chemicals in the bat's saliva keep the blood from clotting. The bat laps up the flowing blood, which follows grooves under its tongue to go down its throat. When it is full, the bat's stomach may be so round that the bat can't take off and fly. Then it will loll about on the ground until some of its food is digested.

The Story of Dracula

The legend of the blood-drinking, un-dead human vampire has its roots in old folktales of eastern Europe. Bram Stoker's novel *Dracula*, published in 1897, gave the story new life. Its main character—a courtly vampire named Count Dracula—has since been the subject of many movies.

What Is a Primate?

You are a primate. So are monkeys, great and lesser apes, lemurs, lorises, and pottos. Primates are a large group of monkeylike mammals found around the world. Apes, the biggest members of the group, live in the forests of Africa and Asia. Monkeys live in the warmer parts of Central and South America, Africa, and Asia. Prosimians, the smallest primates, live in Africa and southern Asia.

From the tiny mouse lemur to the massive gorilla, primates have many features in common. These traits show that their ancestors lived in trees. For instance, primates have long, flexible arms and legs. Most have opposable thumbs, allowing them to grasp branches (and tools), and unlike people, the first digits on their hind feet, or big toes, are also opposable. They have binocular vision, meaning that their eyes face forward, giving them a good sense of how far away things are. Most important, perhaps, they have big brains.

So the next time you take your big brain to the zoo, spend a few moments looking at the chimpanzees. Tests of human and chimpanzee cells show that chimps are your closest relatives in the animal world.

Primate Hands

Bush Baby
This small tree-dweller has padded fingers for grabbing slippery surfaces.

Gibbon
A great acrobat, the gibbon has long fingers that easily wrap around branches.

Chimpanzee
Chimpanzees live in the trees and on the ground, too, so their fingers are shorter.

Gorilla
The ground-dwelling gorilla doesn't need long fingers or padded fingertips.

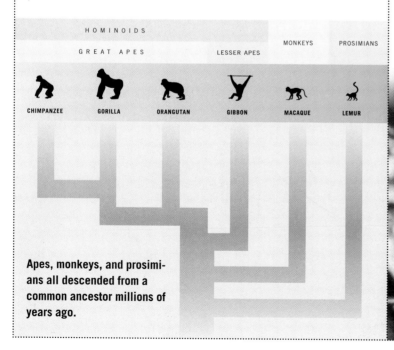

Apes, monkeys, and prosimians all descended from a common ancestor millions of years ago.

HOMINOIDS

GREAT APES   LESSER APES   MONKEYS   PROSIMIANS

CHIMPANZEE   GORILLA   ORANGUTAN   GIBBON   MACAQUE   LEMUR

The largest primate, an adult male gorilla, called a silverback, is shown here shouting at an intruder.

The Brain

Lemur

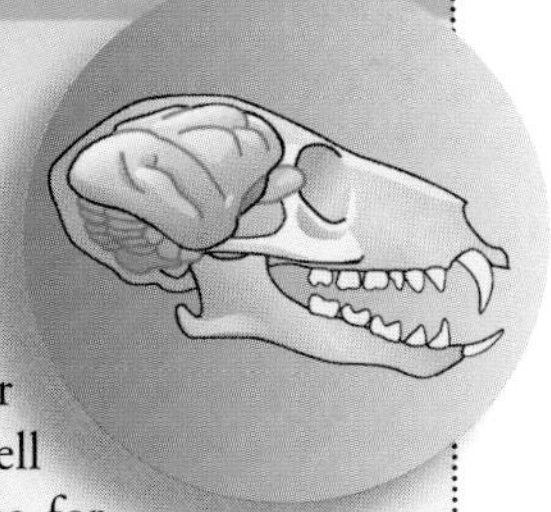

A lemur's brain has a large smell center *(pink)* as well as a big area for the brainstem and instincts *(purple)*.

Human

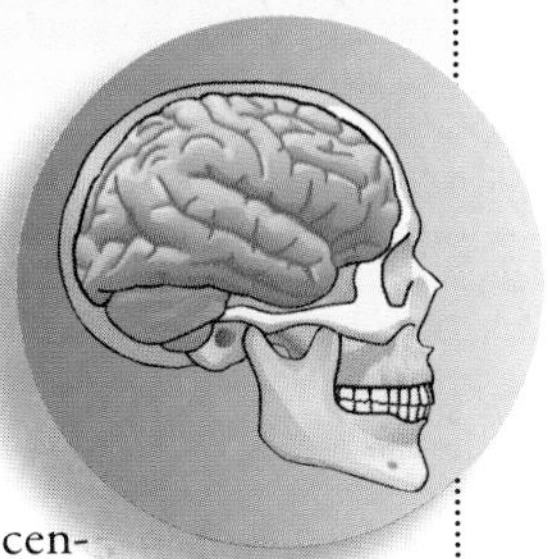

The human brain has a huge cerebrum *(pink)*, the center of reason. The smell center and brainstem area *(purple)* have shrunk.

The Smallest Primate

The lesser mouse lemur—the world's smallest primate—could fit into the palm of your hand. Adult animals average 100 g (3.5 oz.) in weight and are about 10 cm (4 in.) long. These tiny animals usually venture out at night. Their excellent night vision helps them to jump through trees in the dark as they hunt for fruit and insects to eat.

Lemurs Prosimians

Bringing up Baby

The word "lemur" comes from an old Latin word for "ghost." It isn't a bad name for these **prosimians,** the lowest suborder of the primates. Lemurs move quietly, usually at night, and sometimes let out eerie, wailing cries.

Lemurs aren't scary when you see them close up, though. To view them in the wild you would have to go to Madagascar or the nearby Comoro Islands in the Indian Ocean. There, these bushy-tailed animals spend most of their time in trees. Some are fantastic leapers, flinging themselves from treetop to treetop.

Lemurs communicate with a variety of hoots. They will also send messages with scent. When a male ring-tailed lemur wants to drive away another male, he first rubs his tail on the smelly glands under his arms. Then he waves the odorous tail in the other male's face. These are called "stink fights."

A ring-tailed lemur baby clings to its mother's back for months after it is born.

Where in the World?

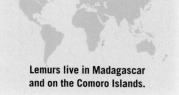

Lemurs live in Madagascar and on the Comoro Islands.

Fast FACTS

Name Ring-tailed lemur

Number of Species 1

Family Lemuridae

Order Primates

Head and Body Length 39-46 cm (1.3-1.5 ft.)

Weight at Maturity 2.3-3.5 kg (5-8 lbs.)

Distribution Southern Madagascar

Habitat Tropical forests; partly terrestrial, in thinly wooded areas

Food Mostly fruits, leaves, and other plant parts; rarely insects

Social Structure Troops of 5-24 where females are dominant and remain in same troop for life; males move between troops

Gestation Period 4.5 months

No. of Young per Pregnancy Usually 1, sometimes 2

Weight at Birth 50-70 g (1.8-2.5 oz.)

Longevity 27 years

Conservation Status Endangered due to rapid deforestation

When a young lemur is about four months old, its mother will begin to feed it solid food, such as fruit.

BUSH BABY

The bush baby is an African relative of the lemur. Perhaps the most striking feature of this sweet-looking primate is its pair of huge, dark eyes. During the day, the pupils of its eyes shrink to narrow slits. For good vision at night, when the bush baby hunts insects and small animals, the pupils expand until they are completely round.

Until a lemur baby is ready for solid food, it will nurse from its mother. Often it will have to share the milk with a twin.

POTTO

Slow and careful, the furry little potto is another African prosimian. It has unusual hands: The index fingers are small stubs, leaving a wide space between the thumb and the other three fingers. This gives the potto an excellent grasp of branches as it climbs. Like most of its relatives, the potto is nocturnal. Creeping about the trees at night, it feeds on fruit and insects. It moves so quietly that it has earned the nickname "softly-softly."

Monkeys Old World and New

New World

When people think of **primates,** they usually think of monkeys. Except for humans, monkeys are the most common and wide-spread primates. They live not only in the jungles of Africa and South America but also as far north as Mexico and Japan.

Scientists put monkeys into two groups: Old World monkeys and New World monkeys. Old World monkeys live in Africa and Asia, while New World monkeys roam the forests from South America through Mexico. You can tell if a monkey is Old World or New World by check-ing its nose, hands, and tail, as shown in the comparison at right. The easiest way to tell them apart is by the tail. Many New World monkeys have **pre-hensile tails,** able to grasp a branch or a tasty piece of fruit. So if you see a monkey hanging by its tail, you know that's an American primate.

Howler monkeys have hollow bones in their throats that make their voices boom. Their cries can be heard for 3 to 5 km (2 to 3 mi.).

HOWLER MONKEY

Spider monkeys are graceful, fast-moving animals. They use their strong prehensile tails as a kind of fifth leg for grasp-ing and balancing.

SPIDER MONKEY

Where in the World?

Monkeys are found mainly in the forests of the Southern Hemisphere.

Let's Compare

Monkeys

	New World	Old World

Hands

Old World monkeys have op-posable thumbs, meaning they can pick up things between thumb and finger; New World monkeys' thumbs move in the same direction as the fingers.

Noses

Old World monkeys have slen-der noses; noses on New World monkeys are broader.

Tails

Most New World monkeys have prehensile tails; Old World monkeys don't.

Fast FACTS

Name New World monkey and Old World monkey

Number of Species 44 New World, 94 Old World

Family 2 families

Order Primates

Head and Body Length 24-89 cm (9-35 in.)

Weight at Maturity 51 g-54 kg (2 oz.-119 lbs.)

Distribution Mexico to Argentina, Africa, Arabian Peninsula, Asia

Habitat Forests, mangroves; Old World monkeys also in savannas

Food Fruits, nuts, leaves, bark; in-sects, small vertebrates, birds' eggs

Social Structure New World: fam-ily groups, some males solitary; Old World: groups of 1 male and several females

Gestation Period 5-7.7 months

No. of Young per Pregnancy 1

Weight at Birth 70-450 g (2.5-16 oz.)

Longevity 12-45 years

Conservation Status Some abun-dant, others endangered

Old World

The proboscis monkey of Borneo has a strange, floppy nose. Only the older males have this odd snout; scientists think the females find the longer noses more attractive. These monkeys like to live near fresh water and swamps.

PROBOSCIS

An Early Space Traveler

In the late 1950s, in the first days of the U.S. space program, four monkeys and two chimps were shot into space to test the safety of spaceflight for humans. The one at left, named Sam, was a rhesus monkey—the kind of monkey that is often used in science experiments. Encased in a "biopack," he rode 88 km (55 mi.) into the upper atmosphere and returned safely.

The Japanese macaque, also known as the snow monkey, is a tough creature. Covered in thick fur, it lives through snowy Japanese winters. Some Japanese macaques like to keep themselves warm by sitting in hot springs.

MACAQUE

Gibbons Lesser Apes

Gibbons are swingers. Long-haired, tailless apes, they are the best tree travelers in the animal kingdom. As they fling themselves hand over hand through the trees, they seem to be flying. Gibbons can also walk upright on the ground, like the great apes. When they do, they hold their long arms high in the air to keep them from dragging in the dirt.

Gibbons are singers, too. Their powerful voices travel for kilometers through the forests of Southeast Asia. At times a male, a female, and their young warble together in a chorus. These sounds help groups of gibbons stay in contact. They also tell unwelcome visitors to go away.

Gibbons stay busy. For most of the day, they swing steadily through the trees, searching for leaves, flowers, fruit, and insects to eat. When darkness falls, the small groups settle down into familiar sleeping trees for a good night's rest.

Where in the World?

Gibbons live on the islands and mainland of Southeast Asia.

Fast FACTS

Name Gibbon

Number of Species 9

Family Hylobatidae

Order Primates

Head and Body Length 44-90 cm (1.4-3 ft.)

Weight at Maturity 4-13 kg (8.8-29 lbs.)

Distribution Southeast Asia from Bangladesh and southernmost China to Malaysia and the islands of Hainan, Sumatra, Java, Borneo

Habitat Trees in deciduous monsoon and evergreen rain forests

Food Fruits, leaves, flowers, insects; small vertebrates, birds' eggs

Social Structure Small family groups

Gestation Period 7-8 months

No. of Young per Pregnancy 1

Weight at Birth Unknown

Longevity About 25 years in the wild

Conservation Status All species endangered due to habitat destruction and illegal hunting

This white-handed gibbon is perfectly comfortable hanging by its powerful arms.

How **Far?** The Gibbon's Powerful Swing

Gibbons move through the trees with an arm-over-arm motion called **brachiation.** In one swing, this ape can travel almost 3 m (10 ft.). Curling their long, narrow fingers, gibbons swing from branch to branch using their hands like hooks, without actually gripping the wood. Family groups may cover nearly a kilometer (.6 mi.) each day, 25 m (80 ft.) up in the trees.

Male and Female Colors

Unlike most other primates, male and female gibbons are not very different in size and shape. Luckily for the scientists who watch them, the males and females often have different coloration. The male white-handed gibbon is mainly black, whereas the female of the pair is ash blond.

Howling Gibbons

Biologists who study gibbons can tell their species just by hearing their loud, melodious calls. Possibly the loudest gibbon of all is the big siamang. This ape has a throat sac that inflates when it calls out. The added throat space adds volume to its booming voice, which can be heard for kilometers through the forest.

Orangutans Great Apes

Fabulous Features!

Orangutans—shy, solitary, and silent—may be the most mysterious of the great apes. Living in the swampy jungles of Borneo and Sumatra, they move quietly through the treetops, their shaggy hair blending into the shadows.

Orangutans spend almost all of their time in trees. They love to eat, so they concentrate on finding the wild figs that ripen in these Asian forests. Heavy adults move carefully through the branches, but the smaller ones swing with ease. Orangutans are not so comfortable on the ground. There, they move slowly, pushing themselves along with their fists to get to the next tree.

Unfortunately, these shy and gentle creatures are **endangered.** Hunting and the loss of their forest habitat have cut their numbers down to a few thousand. They are now protected by law—but they may end up surviving only in zoos.

Four Holds in the Trees

Although orangutans are heavy and sometimes get hurt in a fall, they are well suited for moving through trees. Like gibbons, they move arm over arm through the branches. Unlike gibbons, they go slowly and use their flexible feet to grasp the limbs as well.

Where in the World?

Orangutans live only on the islands of Borneo and Sumatra.

What's a Primatologist?

Primatologists are scientists who study primates. The most famous orangutan primatologist is Biruté Galdikas (left). She has studied wild orangs in Borneo for almost 30 years, patiently tramping through the forest with notebook, binoculars, and a day's rations to observe these shy creatures.

The two babies in the tub, Dr. Galdikas' son Binti and the orang, Princess (right), grew up as playmates in the jungles of Borneo.

Fast FACTS

Name Orangutan

Number of Species 1

Family Pongidae

Order Primates

Head and Body Length 125-150 cm (4-5 ft.)

Weight at Maturity 30-90 kg (66-198 lbs.)

Distribution The islands of Borneo and Sumatra in Indonesia

Habitat Trees in primary forests

Food Mainly fruits, especially figs; some leaves, mineral-rich soil, insects, possibly small vertebrates and birds' eggs

Social Structure Primarily solitary or small groups

Gestation Period 7.5-9 months

No. of Young per Pregnancy 1, rarely 2

Weight at Birth 1.6-1.9 kg (3.5-4.2 lbs.)

Longevity To 59 years in captivity

Conservation Status Endangered by habitat loss and illegal hunting and trapping

Aping Mom

Orangutans have small families. A female will have one baby only every eight or nine years. The little ones then stay with the mother for years, riding on her back and learning to move through the forest. Like other babies, the young orangutans are playful and affectionate. When they are five or six years old, they become more independent and eventually go off on their own.

Orangutan

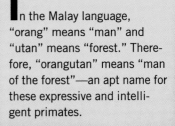

Nesting

When night approaches, orangs build wide platform nests out of branches, high up in the trees. There they sleep safe from predators.

In the Malay language, "orang" means "man" and "utan" means "forest." Therefore, "orangutan" means "man of the forest"—an apt name for these expressive and intelligent primates.

Gorillas Gentle Giants

If they weren't threatened with extinction, you might say that gorillas have an ideal life. Living in small groups called troops, they wander slowly through the forests of central Africa. For about half the day, they search for leaves, vines, and bamboo shoots to eat. For the rest of the time, they laze in the sun and play with their children. On the rare occasion when another gorilla threatens them, the troop's leader, an adult male called a silverback, protects them. He will rear up and beat his chest *(right)* to frighten the intruder away.

Most of the time they are peaceful creatures. Gorillas are the largest of the great apes. Grown male mountain gorillas can weigh more than 225 kg (500 lbs.) and stand almost 1.8 m (6 ft.) tall. Their immensely strong arms can span nearly 3 m (10 ft.). So it's a good thing that they are gentle. Few animals could fight an angry gorilla and survive.

Where in the World?

Gorillas live in central Africa.

Fast FACTS

Name Gorilla

Number of Species 1

Family Pongidae

Order Primates

Head and Body Length 125-175 cm (4.1-5.7 ft.)

Weight at Maturity 70-275 kg (154-605 lbs.)

Distribution Equatorial West Africa and Rwanda, Uganda, and Congo

Habitat Lowland tropical forests, montane rain forests, and bamboo forests

Food Mainly leaves, shoots, and stems; less often wood, flowers, fruits, and grubs

Social Structure Groups of 1 or 2 adult males, a few subadult males, several females, and young

Gestation Period 8-9.5 months

No. of Young per Pregnancy 1, rarely 2

Weight at Birth 2 kg (4.4 lbs.)

Longevity Up to 50 years in the wild; 54 years in captivity

Conservation Status Endangered

Gorillas nest on the ground.

Gorillas sleep in nests that they build on the ground. At the end of the day, each adult gorilla will spend a few minutes putting together a soft, flat platform from leaves, branches, and moss. The young gorillas sleep in the mother's nest.

I Was There!

For 20 years primatologist Dian Fossey studied gorillas in the mountains of Rwanda, Africa. When she began her observations, the gorillas ran from her. In time they accepted her being near them.

One day, after more than three years of watching them, she noticed a curious young male approaching her. She had seen him often and had named him Peanuts. Hoping for closer contact, she held out her hand palm up because the palms of a human and a gorilla are more similar than the back of the hand.

"Peanuts seemed to ponder accepting my hand," she later wrote. "Finally he came a step closer and, extending his own hand, gently touched his fingers to mine." This was probably the first time that a wild gorilla voluntarily touched a human. In typical gorilla fashion Peanuts expressed his excitement for being so daring by beating his chest. Then he rejoined his group.

"I expressed my own happy excitement by crying," Dian Fossey wrote. Soon after that the animals in the troop became her friends.

Child Care

Gorilla babies cling to their mothers from the time they are only a few hours old until about three years.

Chimpanzees Party Animals

A generation ago we knew almost nothing about chimpanzees, our closest relatives in the animal world. Today, we are much closer to understanding their complex lives, thanks mainly to one person: Jane Goodall.

This English **primatologist** spent her childhood watching animals and writing about them in a journal. By the time she was 20, she had set out for Tanzania, in Africa. Because she was so young, the authorities made her take her mother with her. She was the first person in 30 years to study chimpanzees in the wild. Very soon, she made two amazing discoveries about chimps: that they made tools, and that they ate meat. Since then, she has seen them adopt orphaned infants and dance with awe in front of a waterfall. In good ways and bad, she has shown that chimps resemble humans more than we ever suspected.

Where in the World?

Chimpanzees live in east, west, and central Africa.

Fast FACTS

Name Chimpanzee

Number of Species 2

Family Pongidae

Order Primates

Head and Body Length 64-94 cm (2-3 ft.)

Weight at Maturity 26-70 kg (57-154 lbs.)

Distribution Equatorial Africa

Habitat Tropical rain forests, savannas, and montane forests

Food Mainly fruits, leaves, blossoms, seeds, stems, bark, resin, honey; also insects, birds' eggs, and meat

Social Structure Large, unstable groups called communities share a home range

Gestation Period 6.5-8.4 months

No. of Young per Pregnancy 1, rarely 2

Weight at Birth 1.9 kg (4.2 lbs.)

Longevity Up to 60 years in the wild

Conservation Status Endangered

Grooming

Chimpanzees spend a lot of time with other chimps from their group, acting up, playing, and chatting. Sometimes they will groom each other. Combing through each other's fur, they pick out dirt and insects. Grooming helps chimps feel comfortable and friendly.

Nesting

At night, chimpanzees sleep in nests that they make on tree branches. Bending twigs and tucking in leaves, they make a soft platform to rest in. This keeps them safe from enemies on the ground.

Acceptance

When Jane Goodall first came to Tanzania, the chimps ran away from her in fear. In time, they came to know her and accept her presence. Here, an 11-month-old baby chimpanzee she named Flint reaches out to her.

Chimpanzees Close up

After many years in the wild, Jane Goodall became the world's leading expert on chimpanzees. Because she is an honest researcher, Goodall sometimes has had to report unpleasant things about chimpanzees. They are capable of "murder," for instance. Females have been seen to kill defenseless infants. Goodall has also seen groups of chimpanzees make war on others. "When I first started at Gombe, I thought the chimpanzees were nicer than we are," she once said. "But time has revealed that they are not. They can be just as awful."

Since 1985, Goodall has spent much of her time raising money to support ape research and conservation. She has also fought for better conditions for laboratory animals. Her example has inspired thousands of young people to become biologists themselves.

Today Jane Goodall still keeps up with her chimp friends. She lectures widely on what she learned in her nearly 40 years of research and also on conservation.

Chimpanzees use tools in several different ways. They will pick up rocks to crack palm nuts for a meal *(below)*. They also strip down twigs and stick them into termite mounds to collect a crunchy insect snack *(below left)*.

Tool Use

Thinking Skills

Communication

Chimpanzees show emotions in their faces. This expression, accompanied by hoots, means that a chimp has found food.

Quick Drinking Thinking

Chimpanzees can think ahead and solve problems. After dipping a stick in a spring, the chimp above licks off the water droplets. Another chimpanzee at left is drinking from a sponge it has made from crushed leaves. The chimp first chewed up the leaves, then dipped them in rainwater and squeezed the water into its mouth.

This scowling face, with lips compressed, shows annoyance and means the chimpanzee may attack.

A chimp that is lower in the social order may bare its teeth when it is afraid or is approaching a more dominant chimp.

What Is a Marsupial?

A marsupial's life starts with a frightening test. When they are born, marsupial babies are tiny, naked, deaf, and blind. Still, in the next four minutes they must drag themselves, inch by inch, over their mother's belly to a pouch of skin. Once inside, they latch onto a teat and start to drink milk. From that time on, they must feel like they're in heaven. They spend weeks or months growing, resting, and eating in mom's pouch while she carries them around.

Marsupials are famous for their pouches. With the exception of the shy opossum from the Americas, these mammals are found mainly in Australia and New Guinea. They include the snarling Tasmanian devil of Tasmania and the cuddly koala of Australia. There are marsupial moles, marsupial mice, marsupial rats, and airborne gliding marsupials. But the best-known marsupial is surely the kangaroo.

Kangaroos are the great leapers of the animal world. When they're just ambling along, grazing and browsing on plants, they have a "five-legged" walk: They hold themselves on their small forelegs and big tail while pulling their hind legs along. When they're leaping in open country—watch out! Their enormous, powerful hind legs fling them along in huge bounds at up to 48 km/h (30 mph). Scientists have discovered that kangaroos are so well designed that they actually use less energy in their giant jumps than other animals use when running.

Where in the World?

Marsupials are found in Australia, nearby islands, and the Americas.

Fast FACTS

Name Kangaroo

Number of Species 3

Family Macropodidae

Order Marsupialia

Head and Body Length 85-160 cm (2.8-5.2 ft.)

Weight at Maturity 20-90 kg (44-198 lbs.)

Distribution Australia and Tasmania

Habitat Gray kangaroos in forests and woodlands; red kangaroos in grassy plains or savannas

Food Grasses

Social Structure Organized groups of 2-10 or more called mobs

Gestation Period 30-36 days in uterus, 7.6-10.3 months in pouch

No. of Young per Pregnancy 1, rarely 2

Weight at Birth .75 g (.03 oz.) when leaving uterus; 2-4 kg (4.4-8.8 lbs.) when leaving pouch

Longevity 20 years in the wild

Conservation Status Relatively common, but may be threatened

Ooof! Ouch!

Male kangaroos (known as "boomers") sometimes have fights that combine wrestling, boxing, kicking, and just standing around. They will punch with their forelegs, shove each other backward, and kick with their powerful hind legs. The loser hops away.

A family of red kangaroos grazes on grasses and other plants along the ground.

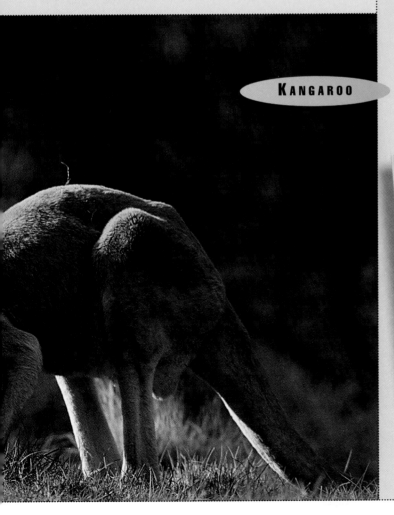

KANGAROO

The Path to the Pouch

Just before her baby is born, the mother kangaroo licks a path along her belly up to the pouch *(above right)*. Sniffing along the path, the baby climbs upward and into the pouch *(right)*. Once arrived, the baby will suckle on a teat *(above)* for its food.

How **Far?**

Fast-moving kangaroos jump an average of 9 m (30 ft.) per bound, but are known to have leaped as far as 13.5 m (44 ft.).

The farthest a human has ever jumped is 8.95 m (29 ft., 4½ in.) in the track and field world championships in Tokyo, Japan, in 1991. No one has jumped farther since then.

Kangaroos are the famous marsupials, but they have lots of smaller, oddball relatives. Take, for instance, the Tasmanian devil. This doglike creature prowls the hills of Tasmania, a large island off the southern coast of Australia. Known for its loud, whining snarl, the devil gobbles down dead wallabies, rabbits, and sheep. Or, there's the beaver-sized wombat. A shy, shuffling animal, the wombat lives in 30-meter-long (100 ft.) tunnels, avoiding company and eating grass, roots, and bark.

But for sheer cuddly charm, nothing beats the koala. Although some people call it the koala bear, it is no bear, but a marsupial. Koalas lead a quiet life of climbing trees and munching eucalyptus leaves. Unfortunately, there aren't as many koalas left as in times past. Disease and loss of habitat have brought their numbers down from millions to a few hundred thousand. Koalas are now protected by law.

KOALA

Where in the World?

Koalas live only in Australia.

Fast FACTS

Name Koala

Number of Species 1

Family Phascolarctidae

Order Marsupialia

Head and Body Length 60-85 cm (2-3 ft.)

Weight at Maturity 4-15 kg (9-33 lbs.)

Distribution Eastern and southern Australia

Habitat Eucalyptus forests

Food Eucalyptus leaves and bark

Social Structure Mainly solitary

Gestation Period 35 days internally, 5-7 months in pouch

No. of Young per Pregnancy 1, rarely 2

Weight at Birth 1 g (.04 oz.)

Longevity 10-20 years

Conservation Status Strictly protected; forest fires, disease, and killing for its warm, durable fur, plus clearing of woodland habitat and human encroachment on habitat, have reduced the formerly large population

Down and Out of the Pouch

Leg first, a baby koala struggles out of the pouch *(left)*. Unlike many marsupials, koalas have a pouch that opens to the rear. A newborn lives in the mother's pouch for seven months, then it rides on the mother's back until it is a year old.

Noisy Devils

TASMANIAN DEVIL

It's difficult to believe they're related to koalas, but Tasmanian devils are marsupials, too, as is the cartoon Taz. Their eerie growls can be heard for miles.

Riding High

SUGAR GLIDER

Sugar gliders are marsupials of the air. Between their front and hind legs is a flap of skin that lets them glide from tree to tree for more than 30 m (100 ft.). They are named for the sweetness of their foods, which include flower nectar, sap, and blossoms.

American Cousins

OPOSSUM

Opossums are found in North and South America. They are active mainly in the evening and at night, climbing on trees with the help of their **prehensile** tail. When threatened, opossums will "play possum,"—that is, they will lie motionless and pretend to be dead. This may fool their enemies into going away.

Picky Eaters

Koalas are among the pickiest eaters in the world. They only eat the leaves and soft bark of certain kinds of eucalyptus trees. Their finicky appetite is one reason why koalas are hard to keep in captivity and are rarely seen in zoos.

Egg-laying Platypus

Fabulous **Features!**

Of all the odd mammals in the world, the platypus may be the oddest. Although the furry animal nurses its young like other mammals, it has a bill like a duck's, and its young hatch from soft, rubbery eggs. When English scientists first saw a platypus skin in 1789, they thought someone was playing a trick on them. They believed a prankster must have sewn together the parts of other animals—the bill of a duck, the tail of a beaver, and the fine fur of a mole.

The animal was real, however. The platypus and its relative, the echidna, are the only two egg-laying mammals, or **monotremes,** in the world. Platypuses live in burrows near ponds and rivers of the southeastern coast of Australia and on the Australian island of Tasmania. Echidnas live in burrows and hollow logs in Australia, Tasmania, and New Guinea.

Where in the World?

Platypuses and echidnas live in Australia, Tasmania, and New Guinea.

Spur

The male platypus has a hollow spur on each hind foot that is connected to poison glands within the legs. The poison can kill another platypus, or even a dog, if it is stabbed in a fight.

Webbed Feet

Platypuses have webbed feet, whose skin extends beyond their toenails. These feet help platypuses dive and swim in the streams and lakes where they find their food. The skin folds under when they walk on the ground.

Bill

The platypus's bill has special sensors, called electroreceptors, that find electric fields made by moving prey in the water. The sensors help the swimming platypus detect and snap up crayfish, snails, worms, tadpoles, and fish.

Fast FACTS

Name Platypus

Number of Species 1

Family Ornithorhynchidae

Order Monotremata

Head and Body Length 30-45 cm (1-1.5 ft.)

Weight at Maturity .5-2 kg (1-4 lbs.)

Distribution Eastern Australia

Habitat Freshwater streams, lakes, and lagoons

Food Crayfish, shrimp, larvae of water insects, snails, tadpoles, worms, and small fish

Social Structure Pairs; male and female live in separate burrows during breeding

Gestation Period 14 days internally, then 10-day incubation period

No. of Young per Pregnancy 1-3

Weight at Birth Less than 3 g (.11 oz.)

Longevity 10 years in the wild, 17 years in captivity

Conservation Status Vulnerable due to habitat disruption

Relatives

ECHIDNA

They don't look much alike, but the echidna is the platypus's closest relative. Also known as the spiny anteater, the echidna has a long, tubelike snout and spiny fur like a hedgehog. It lives on land and eats termites and ants. The female incubates her eggs in a pouch on her belly.

With its streamlined body and webbed feet, the platypus is a good swimmer. It can stay underwater for up to five minutes.

The Platypus's Home

When she is ready to lay her eggs, the female platypus carries wet leaves to a nesting chamber at the end of a long, winding burrow. Like a bird, she curls around her eggs and keeps them warm for 10 days. When the babies hatch—only 25 mm (1 in.) long—they climb onto her belly and lap up milk from openings in her skin.

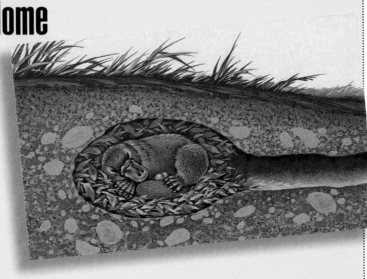

Leathery Eggs

The eggs of the platypus, shown actual size above, look and feel different from chicken eggs. They are rounder and have a tough, leathery shell. The female will lay between one and three eggs. The eggs will stick together so they cannot roll away.

What Are Sea Mammals?

Sea mammals dwell in the vast world of the oceans and coastal waterways. They are warm-blooded, have hair on their bodies, breathe air through lungs, and nurse their young, the same as land mammals. Millions of years ago they even lived on land. Today sea mammals live in the water, where they get their food, and have evolved flippers, fins, and flukes to equip them for underwater life.

The three groups of sea mammals—Pinnipedia (seals, sea lions, and walruses), Cetacea (whales, dolphins, and porpoises), and Sirenia (manatees and dugongs)—are remarkably diverse. Pinnipeds live in water and reproduce on land; their legs have turned into flippers, and they have a hairy coat to protect them. Cetaceans look similar to fish and live entirely at sea, though they must come to the surface to breathe. Sirenians are almost hairless and have paddlelike forelimbs but no hind limbs.

All three groups are hunted for their meat and blubber—the coating of fat that keeps them warm in icy waters. Many whales have come close to extinction, but conservation groups are ensuring their protection.

Let's Compare

One way to tell the difference between whales and fish is to look at the tail. Fish have vertical fins that move from side to side. The mammals' flukes are horizontal and move up and down in a "power stroke."

Fish

Sea Mammal

Kayakers get an eyeful of a humpback's mighty flukes. Although whales are normally harmless, boaters have to be careful: An accidental blow from their enormous tail would crush a small boat.

A Whale Is Born: Underwater

Two seconds after its birth, with the blood still billowing through the water, a baby beluga whale heads to the surface to take its first breath. Then it will return to its mother to nurse.

Baleen Whales

Fabulous Features!

There are two suborders of whales: toothed and baleen. Except for the sperm whale, which is toothed, all the largest whales are baleen, including the blue whale—the largest animal ever. "Baleen" refers to the thin **keratin** plates that grow in the whale's mouth instead of teeth and act like a strainer for catching food. Sturdy but flexible, baleen was called whalebone by 19th-century hunters, who sold it for use in corsets, hoop skirts, and umbrellas. These enormous whales subsist on a diet of tiny shrimplike plankton called krill. They need no particular defenses, as their size keeps them from having many natural enemies.

Whales live in the oceans but breathe through lungs and must come to the surface for air. They exchange air through blowholes on top of their head—baleen whales have two, toothed whales have one—which they close before diving.

Displaying a wide row of **baleen,** a southern right whale swims open-mouthed to gulp seawater rich with krill. As the whale forces out the water with its huge tongue, the krill are trapped in the baleen, and the whale can lick off its meal.

Where in the World?

Baleen whales swim in all the oceans of the world.

Would You Believe?

Gone Fishin'

Humpback whales catch fish with a "bubble net." They surround the fish and blow bubbles, frightening the fish into the middle of the "net," where they are easy prey.

Fast FACTS

Name Baleen whale

Number of Species 10

Family 4 families

Order Cetacea

Head and Body Length 5.5-31 m (18-102 ft.)

Weight at Maturity 2,850-160,000 kg (6,300-350,000 lbs.)

Distribution All oceans, salt water seas, and bays of the world

Habitat Mainly found in the open sea; gray whale frequents shallow waters close to shore

Food Krill, copepods, small squid, fish. Gray whale takes small mollusks, worms, and fish from sandy bottom sediments

Social Structure Alone or small groups of 2-10; hundreds may gather at abundant food source

Gestation Period 10-13 months

No. of Young per Pregnancy 1

Weight at Birth 500-2,000 kg (1,100-4,400 lbs.)

Longevity About 46-114 years

Conservation Status Endangered

A humpback whale bursts out of the sea to catch a breath of air before crashing back into the water, a practice known as "breaching."

How Big?

Blue whales are the biggest animals that ever lived. They grow to about 30 m (100 ft.) long and weigh around 150,000 kg (330,000 lbs.)—as much as 22 elephants.

People Roger Payne

In a motorboat off the coast of Alaska, Roger Payne *(far left)* records the sounds of humpback whales. Dr. Payne is regarded as one of the world's top cetacean biologists. More than 30 years ago he dedicated himself to preserving the world's shrinking whale populations. He discovered and recorded the songs that humpback whales compose for one another to communicate and perhaps use as a mating call. The humpbacks' haunting songs helped gain popular support for whale conservation. Since then, Dr. Payne has been conducting a continuous study of a group of right whales.

Toothed Whales

Fabulous Features!

The six families in the suborder of toothed whales include whales, dolphins, and porpoises—all with different teeth. The sperm whale has teeth only on its lower jaw that fit into sockets in the upper jaw when the mouth is closed. These teeth work well for catching squid. Dolphins and killer whales have teeth in both upper and lower jaws. Their diet consists mainly of fish, although killer whales will tackle larger mammals as well.

All of these animals' habitats vary greatly. Some live only far out at sea. Killer whales are seen both in deep ocean waters and inshore. They are the fastest sea mammal, speeding through the ocean at 45 km/h (28 mph). Sperm whales can dive deeper and stay submerged longer than any other mammal—up to 40 minutes at a time. And some dolphins inhabit only rivers.

Killer Teeth

A killer whale, or orca, flashes a mouthful of pointed teeth shaped to hold slippery food such as fish and squid.

Where in the World?

Toothed whales swim in all oceans and seas.

Fast FACTS

Name Toothed whale

Number of Species 30

Family 6 families

Order Cetacea

Head and Body Length 210 cm–15.2 m (6.9–50 ft.)

Weight at Maturity 136–50,000 kg (300–110,230 lbs.)

Distribution All oceans and seas

Habitat Coastal waters to deep, open ocean

Food Mostly squid, sharks, fish, crustaceans; killer whales also eat seals, young walruses, dolphins, and penguins

Social Structure Usually groups of 2-40 or large gatherings of several hundred

Gestation Period 11-17 months

No. of Young per Pregnancy 1

Weight at Birth 180-1,000 kg (397-2,205 lbs.)

Longevity 25-77 years

Conservation Status Sperm whale endangered, others abundant

What's an Albino?

An albino is an animal lacking in skin and hair color, which makes it appear completely white, and it usually has pink eyes. True albinos are extremely rare, such as the calf (above) seen in the North Atlantic in the spring of 1995. The haunting appearance of an albino sperm whale in the 19th century may have been the inspiration for Herman Melville's *Moby Dick,* the novel about a fierce white sperm whale that attacked whaling boats and was pursued by mad Captain Ahab.

Resting before the next hunt, killer whales line up like a squadron of warplanes.

Whale Survival

Whale Rescue

With poles and chain saws, an international team of rescue workers frantically chipped through ice in Point Barrow, Alaska, to free three trapped gray whales in October 1988. The whales were caught under 60 cm (2 ft.) of ice and could not come up to breathe. When the ice continued to thicken, a Russian icebreaker plowed a path so the whales could escape.

Hit the Beach

A killer whale nearly comes ashore in pursuit of a sea lion, one of its favorite preys. Killer whales are the only cetaceans that eat other mammals. Despite their scary name, killer whales are not known to ever have killed a human.

Dolphins and Porpoises

Most people don't realize that dolphins and porpoises are toothed whales, too, only smaller ones, with a single blowhole. The dolphin family is the largest among the cetaceans, comprising more than 40 species.

Humans have grown closer to dolphins than to any other sea creature because of the dolphin's playful nature. They follow complicated instructions, such as fetching objects of a specific color, and can remember strings of random numbers. Researchers are convinced that dolphins are as intelligent as chimpanzees.

Dolphins move swiftly, swimming in tight formations. They can defend themselves in a group with their pointed snouts and teeth to discourage even hungry sharks. The greatest single threat to dolphins, sadly, is the fishing net, which often entangles them when boats drag for fish.

Where in the World?

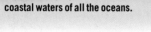

Dolphins and porpoises live in the coastal waters of all the oceans.

Echolocation

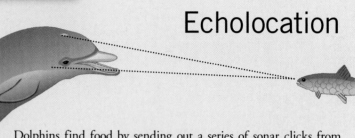

Dolphins find food by sending out a series of sonar clicks from their nasal cavity. The echoes of the clicks bounce off the fish and come back to the dolphin's inner ear to guide it to the prey.

Joy Ride

A boy frolics with a pink dolphin in the water at Oasis Sea World in Bangkok, Thailand. Sometimes, even in the wild, the playful dolphins seek out human playmates.

River Dolphin

The Chinese river dolphin is almost blind because it doesn't need its eyes for finding food in the cloudy river water where it lives.

Fast FACTS

Name Dolphin and Porpoise

Number of Species 41

Family 6 families

Order Cetacea

Head and Body Length 110-400 cm (3.6-13 ft.)

Weight at Maturity 25-450 kg (55-992 lbs.)

Distribution All oceans and seas, bays, estuaries; some inland rivers

Habitat Fresh or salt water in ocean, coastal waters, straits, estuaries, fjords, large rivers

Food Mainly fish, squid, octopus, and crustaceans

Social Structure Usually in groups of 5 to several hundred

Gestation Period 10-12 months

No. of Young per Pregnancy 1

Weight at Birth 6-12 kg (13.2-26.5 lbs.)

Longevity Usually 6-40 years

Conservation Status Some populations are stable, but many species are endangered or threatened by past or current hunting

Bottlenose Dolphins

Seals and Walruses

Seals and walruses spend a lot of time on land. Although these sea mammals are more at home in the water, they come ashore to sleep, mate, and bear their young.

Seals belong to the order Pinnipedia, meaning "fin-footed." They can use their **flippers** as feet when they want to walk. Of the three families of seals—eared seals (sea lions and fur seals), earless seals, and walruses—earless seals make up the majority of species and are called "true seals." All are terrific swimmers and deep divers. Their sleek bodies and powerful flippers make them well adapted to life in the ocean, where they feed and play. The blubber—a thick lining of fat under the skin—and fur that protect seals and walruses in their polar environment have also made them preferred targets of hunters.

Where in the World?

Seals and walruses live along the coasts and islands as shown in dark green.

Let's Compare

Seals

Eared   **Earless**

Eared seals, such as sea lions, can turn their hind flippers forward to function like feet on sand and ice. They can move better on land than earless seals, which must slither along like giant worms.

Earless seals use their hind flippers to swim; eared seals use their long front flippers for power and hind flippers only to steer.

Watchful Walrus

Second in size only to the elephant seal, the distinctive walrus has a bristly mustache, used for finding shellfish, and ivory tusks that grow up to 1 m (3 ft.) long, used in fighting and climbing onto ice. The walrus lives mainly near the moving pack ice of the Arctic Ocean.

WALRUS

Fast FACTS

Name Seal and Walrus

Number of Species 34

Family 3 families

Order Pinnipedia

Head and Body Length 110-600 cm (3.6-19.7 ft.)

Weight at Maturity 27-3,700 kg (59-8,157 lbs.)

Distribution All seacoasts, islands, inland seas

Habitat Arctic, temperate, and subtropical waters along seacoasts; rocky islands, sandy beaches, and ice floes

Food Krill, squid, fish, other prey

Social Structure Breeding colonies may have up to a million seals

Gestation Period 9-12 months

No. of Young per Pregnancy 1, rarely 2

Weight at Birth 3-63 kg (6.6-139 lbs.)

Longevity For most, 20-30 years

Conservation Status Several species are endangered or extinct; most populations are stable

Trumpeting Elephant Seal

True to its name, the elephant seal has a trunklike nose, which helps it shout out a threatening roar that can be heard for nearly a kilometer. It is the largest of all seals. Bull elephant seals can grow to 6 m (20 ft.) long and weigh more than four tons.

King of the Beach

Male sea lions are known to be ill-tempered, especially during mating season. A bull must guard a harem of a dozen females, often fighting off rival suitors.

Last One In...!

Shouting and barking uproariously, seals dive in for a group swim. Seals gather in large numbers along the rocks, beaches, and ice floes near the Arctic and Antarctic circles.

Mild-mannered Manatees

Large and lumbering manatees with whiskered snouts, front flippers, and paddle-shaped tails are plant-eating sea mammals, often called sea cows. Three manatee species and the single dugong make up the small order Sirenia, so called because they were once thought to be the sirens, or mermaids, of myth.

Sirenians are the only vegetarian sea mammals, and their steady feeding on sea grasses helps keep coastal waterways unclogged. Ironically, their leisurely pace of feeding in warm, shallow waters and rivers often makes manatees victims of boaters, who benefit most from their grass-clearing. To protect these peaceful creatures, the state of Florida has created sanctuaries where injured manatees are healed and others are kept safe from deathly powerboat propeller blades. These special sanctuaries help ensure that the endangered manatees will not become extinct.

Where in the World?

Manatees live in coastal waters and rivers, as shown in blue.

Fast FACTS

Name Manatee

Number of Species 3

Family Trichechidae

Order Sirenia

Head and Body Length 250-450 cm (8-14 ft.)

Weight at Maturity 200-600 kg (440-1,323 lbs.)

Distribution Coastal waters and rivers of North, Central, and South America; West Africa

Habitat Shallow coastal waters, estuaries, lagoons, rivers, swamps

Food Aquatic plants

Social Structure North American species seen alone or in small family groups; Amazon and African species in large groups

Gestation Period 12-13 months

No. of Young per Pregnancy 1

Weight at Birth 28-36 kg (62-79 lbs.)

Longevity 13 years in the wild; up to 30 years in captivity

Conservation Status Vulnerable or endangered

Playful manatees engage in an underwater waltz as adults and calves tumble around, using their flippers like hands.

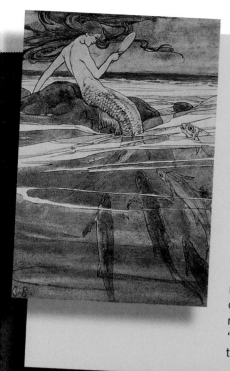

That's a Mermaid?

For centuries sailors thought that manatees, with their fish-like tails and almost human faces, were the mermaids described in legend. Even Christopher Columbus, after spotting manatees in the Caribbean, claimed he had seen three mermaids, though he added that "they were not as beautiful as they are painted."

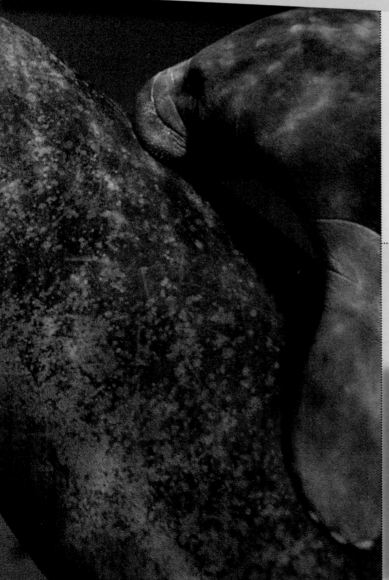

Relatives

DUGONG

The dugongs of the Indian Ocean and Australia's ocean shoals are smaller and have a divided, flukelike tail. They live only in salt water, whereas manatees are found in fresh water as well.

Restored to Health

Munching on a water hyacinth, a manatee still shows scars from propeller blades. It was sent to a sanctuary in Florida to heal and was released only when danger from infection had passed.

Flipper Food

Manatees nurse their young through a teat behind their flippers for about two years. On rare occasions, a mother will nurse a newborn and an older calf on each side.

Picture Credits

The sources for the illustrations are listed below. Credits from left to right are separated by semicolons, from top to bottom by dashes.

Cover: book spine, ©Tim Davis/Photo Researchers; front, Merlin D. Tuttle, Bat Conservation International; Rinie Van Meurs/Bruce Coleman Collection, Uxbridge, Middlesex—Yann Arthus-Bertrand; art by Jerry Lofaro.

All maps and silhouettes by John Drummond, Time Life Inc.

Title page: Art by Will Nelson/Northwest Arts, Ltd. 4: Kenneth W. Fink/Ardea Limited, London—Silvestris/FLPA, Wetheringsett, Suffolk—art by Maria DiLeo. 5: Art by Linda Nye; Leonard Lee Rue III—©John Giustina/The Wildlife Collection; Daryl Balfour/NHPA, Ardingly, Sussex. 6: (Art) Will Nelson/Northwest Arts, Ltd. (3)—Cori Zeller; Will Nelson/Northwest Arts, Ltd. 7: (Art) Will Nelson/Northwest Arts, Ltd.—Cori Zeller (2)—Will Nelson/Northwest Arts, Ltd. (2). 8: Art by Heather Lovett. 9: J. P. Scott/Planet Earth Pictures, London. 10, 11: Des & Jen Bartlet/Survival Anglia, Oxford Scientific Films, Long Hanborough, Oxfordshire; Michael Gore/Nature Photographers, Little London, Hampshire; art by Heather Lovett—Mary Evans Picture Library, London. 12: Art by Robin DeWitt—Anup & Manoj Shah/Planet Earth Pictures, London. 13: Art by Stephen R. Wagner; Olivier Blaise, Gamma Liaison—©Christian Grzimek/Oxford Scientific Films, Long Hanborough, Oxfordshire—Mary Evans Picture Library, London; ©E. Hanumantha Rao/NHPA, Ardingly, Sussex. 14, 15: ©Tom McHugh, The National Audubon Society Collection/Photo Researchers; Douglas Chadwick—art by Heather Lovett; Jeff Foott Productions/Bruce Coleman Collection, Uxbridge, Middlesex. 16, 17: Art Wolfe, Inc.; art by Will Nelson/Northwest Arts, Ltd.—art by Maria DiLeo; Johnny Johnson/Bruce Coleman Collection, Uxbridge, Middlesex; Leonard Lee Rue III/Bruce Coleman Collection, Uxbridge, Middlesex; art by Maria DiLeo. 18: Jane Burton/Bruce Coleman Collection, Uxbridge, Middlesex; Kit Houghton Photography, Spaxton, Somerset—Jean-Paul Ferrero/Ardea Limited, London; Kit Houghton Photography, Spaxton, Somerset—Gerard Lacz/NHPA, Ardingly, Sussex; Kit Houghton Photography, Spaxton, Somerset. 19: ©David Alan Harvey/Magnum Photos, Inc.; ©Tomas D. W. Friedmann/Photo Researchers—art by Linda Nye. 20: Kenneth W. Fink/Ardea Limited, London—Wendy Dennis/Planet Earth Pictures, London—B. Gibbs/Natural Science Photos, Watford, Hertfordshire. 21: Anthony Bannister/NHPA, Ardingly, Sussex; R. F. Porter/Ardea Limited, London; photography by Jessie Cohen, National Zoological Park, Smithsonian Institution—Steve Bloom/Planet Earth Pictures, London. 22, 23: Alan Root/Oxford Scientific Films, Long Hanborough, Oxfordshire; Jean Jacques Grezet/Jacana, Paris—©Trevor Barrett/Bruce Coleman Collection, Uxbridge, Middlesex; Mike Pattisall (notebook paper)—Mary Plage/Oxford Scientific Films, Long Hanborough, Oxfordshire; ©Anthony Bannister/NHPA, Ardingly, Sussex—Brinsley Burbidge/Nature Photographers, Little London, Hampshire. 24, 25: ©Tom Hollyman/Photo Researchers (background). Kenneth W. Fink/Ardea Limited, London (2)—art by Linda Nye; art by Robin DeWitt (2); art by Will Nelson/Northwest Arts, Ltd.—art by Heather Lovett (2). 26, 27: François Gohier/Nature; François Gohier/Pho.n.e. (2)—Transparency #3886, courtesy Department of Library Services, American Museum of Natural History—Loren McIntyre. 28: PhotoSafari (PVT) Ltd./Natural Science Photos, Watford, Hertfordshire;

art by Linda Nye—art by Will Nelson/Northwest Arts, Ltd.—Gordon Langsbury/Bruce Coleman Collection, Uxbridge, Middlesex. 29: Ferrero-Labat/Ardea Limited, London; Rainon Alain/Jacana, Paris—art by Will Nelson/Northwest Arts, Ltd. 30: ©Press-Tige Pictures/Oxford Scientific Films, Long Hanborough, Oxfordshire—art by Heather Lovett. 31: ©Stephen Krasemann/NHPA, Ardingly, Sussex—Velma Harris; art by Will Nelson/Northwest Arts, Ltd. 32, 33: Dominique and Serge Simon; François Gohier/Nature—Mandal Ranjit/NHPA, Ardingly, Sussex—Werner Layer/Jacana, Paris; ©Leonard Lee Rue III/Photo Researchers; Paal Hermansen/NHPA, Ardingly, Sussex. 34, 35: Leonard Lee Rue III; ©Lowell Georgia/Photo Researchers—©Ken Cole/Natural Science Photos, Watford, Hertfordshire; art by Heather Lovett—George F. Mobley/National Geographic Society Image Collection—art by Robin DeWitt. 36, 37: Judy Cooney/Oxford Scientific Films, Long Hanborough, Oxfordshire; Peter Craig-Cooper/Nature Photographers, Little London, Hampshire; M. P. Kahl/Bruce Coleman Collection, Uxbridge, Middlesex—M & C Denis-Hout/Planet Earth Pictures, London; art by Robin DeWitt; ©Mitch Reardon/Photo Researchers—Daryl Balfour/NHPA, Ardingly, Sussex. 38: Art by Robin DeWitt—©Francis Mayer/Photo Researchers. 39: AP/Wide World Photos; John Running (inset). 40: ©Martyn Colbeck/Oxford Scientific Films, Long Hanborough, Oxfordshire—art by Linda Nye; ©Van Bucher/Photo Researchers. 41: ©Yann Arthus-Bertrand; ©Lon E. Lauber/Oxford Scientific Films, Long Hanborough, Oxfordshire—J. Hobday/Natural Science Photos, Watford, Hertfordshire; ©François Gohier/Ardea Limited, London. 42: Art by Robin DeWitt—©Roger Tidman/Nature Photographers, Little London, Hampshire—Scott McKinley/Planet Earth Pictures, London. 43: Douglas Chadwick. 44, 45: Rudolf Konig/Jacana, Paris; art by Linda Nye; Yann Arthus-Bertrand. 46, 47: Leonard Lee Rue III; Daryl Balfour/NHPA, Ardingly, Sussex—Des & Jen Bartlett/Oxford Scientific Films, Long Hanborough, Oxfordshire; Beverly Joubert/National Geographic Society Image Collection. 48: Gunter Ziesler/Bruce Coleman Collection, Uxbridge, Middlesex—©Tom McHugh, Photo Researchers/Oxford Scientific Films, Long Hanborough, Oxfordshire—Miriam Austerman/Oxford Scientific Films, Long Hanborough, Oxfordshire. 49: Masahiro Iijima/Ardea Limited, London. 50: Carol Farneti Foster/Natural Science Photos, Watford, Hertfordshire—San Diego Museum of Man. 51: Art by Cori Zeller; Jonathan Scott/Planet Earth Pictures, London—Alan & Sandy Carey/Oxford Scientific Films, Long Hanborough, Oxfordshire; ©Renee Lynn/Oxford Scientific Films, Long Hanborough, Oxfordshire. 52, 53: Mark Webber/Planet Earth Pictures, London; art by John Norris Wood—art by Robin DeWitt—Jonathan Scott/Planet Earth Pictures, London; courtesy of the Trustees of the V & A, London. 54, 55: Leonard Lee Rue III; ©Betty K. Bruce, Animals Animals—Belinda Wright/Oxford Scientific Films, Long Hanborough, Oxfordshire; art by Heather Lovett—Michael Holford, Loughton, Essex; ©John Shaw/NHPA, Ardingly, Sussex. 56, 57: ©John Giustina/The Wildlife Collection; Keren Su/Natural Science Photos, Watford, Hertfordshire—Stefan Meyers/Ardea Limited, London—art by Heather Lovett; ©John Giustina/The Wildlife Collection. 58, 59: François Gohier/Ardea Limited, London; art by John Norris Wood; Masahiro Iijima/Ardea Limited, London—art by Will Nelson/Northwest Arts, Ltd; Leonard Lee Rue III; Johnny Johnson/Bruce Coleman Collection, Uxbridge, Middlesex. 60: François Gohier/Ardea Limited, London—art by Will Nelson/Northwest Arts, Ltd. 61: Dan Guravich/Oxford Scientific Films, Long Hanborough, Oxfordshire (2)—©Syvertsen Ragnar/

Glossary of Terms

Alpha (**al**-fuh) Having the highest rank of its gender in a group —the leader—as in alpha male.

Baleen (bay-**leen**) Sievelike plates in the mouths of certain types of whales that have no teeth; the plates are used for straining food from the water.

Biologist (bye-**ol**-uh-jist) A person who studies living organisms and life processes, including their structure, behavior, growth, origin, evolution, and distribution.

Brachiation (bray-kee-**ay**-shuhn) Swinging by the arms from branch to branch, as certain apes do.

Browser (**brouz**-er) An animal that feeds on leaves, young shoots, and twigs, rather than grazes on grass.

Camouflage (**kam**-uh-flazh) Protective coloration that allows an animal to blend into its environment, reducing its chances of being detected by predators.

Canines (**kay**-nines) The sharp-pointed teeth located on either side of the upper and lower jaws, next to the incisors.

Canopy (**kan**-uh-pee) The high, overarching layer of vegetation in a rain forest; formed by the mass of treetops intertwined with vines and flowering plants.

Carnassials (kar-**nas**-ee-uhls) The last upper premolars and the first lower molar teeth in carnivores, adapted for tearing flesh.

Carnivore (**kar**-nuh-vor) An animal that eats meat.

Carrion (**kair**-ee-un) The flesh of dead animals.

Class (**klass**) A category of biological classification between phylum and order. A class is a group of related orders.

Classification system (klass-uh-fuh-**kay**-shuhn **siss**-tuhm) A system scientists have developed to group organisms together by their natural relationships. The categories, going from the most inclusive to the most specific, are: kingdom, phylum, class, order, family, genus, and species.

Cold-blooded (**kohld**-**bluhd**-id) Lacking the ability to regulate body temperature. The body temperature of a cold-blooded animal fluctuates with that of the surrounding air or water.

Dewclaw (**doo**-klaw) An imperfectly developed toe, claw, or hoof on the foot of certain mammals.

Diurnal (dye-**ur**-nal) Active during the day rather than at night.

Domesticate (doh-**mess**-tuh-kate) To train or adapt an animal to live in a human environment and be of use to humans.

Echolocation (ek-oh-loh-**kay**-shuhn) The process of finding an object by using sound waves, which are reflected off the object and back to the sender.

Emergent layer (ee-**mur**-jent **lay**-ur) The uppermost layer of trees in a rain forest which push above the canopy.

Endangered (en-**dayn**-jurd) A species on the brink of extinction.

Extinct (ek-**stingkt**) No longer existing or living.

Family (**fam**-i-lee) A category of biological classification between genus and order; includes related genera.

Feral (**fair**-uhl) Having returned from domestication to a wild, untamed state.

Fin (**fin**) A limb of an aquatic animal, used to move or guide it.

Flipper (**flip**-ur) A wide, flat limb, as of a seal or whale, adapted especially for swimming.

Fluke (**flook**) One of the lobes of a whale's tail.

Forest floor (**for**-ist flor) The lowest layer of vegetation in a rain forest, usually bare except for fallen leaves, decaying plants, and some sprouting plants.

Genus (**jee**-nuhss) A category of biological classification between family and species. A genus is composed of species that are structurally related.

Gestation (jess-**tay**-shuhn) The length of a pregnancy.

Habitat (**hab**-i-tat) The local environment in which a plant or animal lives.

Herbivore (**hur**-buh-vor) An animal that eats only plant matter.

Hibernation (hye-bur-**nay**-shuhn) A state in which an animal's metabolism slows down for sleep through the winter.

Incisors (in-**sye**-zurs) In mammals the sharp-edged front teeth located between the canine teeth in either jaw and adapted for cutting.

Incubate (**ing**-kyuh-bate) To keep eggs warm by body heat, to promote the development and hatching of young.

Insectivore (in-**sek**-tuh-vor) Any of various mammals of the order Insectivora, "feeding on insects." This order includes the shrews, moles, and hedgehogs.

Invertebrate (in-**vur**-tuh-brate) Lacking a backbone or spinal column.

Keratin (**kair**-uh-tin) A tough, fibrous, protein substance that forms the outer layer of hair, nails, horns, and hoofs.

Kingdom (**king**-duhm) The largest category of biological classification. All living and fossil organisms are divided into five kingdoms: Monera (bacteria), Protista (organisms composed of one—rarely more—cell), Fungi, Plantae, and Animalia.

Lodge (**loj**) The den of certain animals, such as the dome-shaped structure built by beavers.

Marsupial (mar-**soo**-pee-uhl) A mammal of the order Marsupialia, including kangaroos, opossums, bandicoots, and wombats; found in Australia and the Americas.

Matriarch (**may**-tree-ark) A female who rules or dominates a group.

Microorganism (mye-kroh-**or**-guh-niz-uhm) An animal or plant of microscopic size, especially a bacterium or a protozoan.

Migration (mye-**gray**-shuhn) The periodic movement of groups of animals to a location with a more favorable climate or more abundant food.

Monotreme (**mon**-uh-treem) Any of an order of egg-laying mammals found in Australia and New Guinea, and including the platypus and echidna.

Montane forest (**mon**-tane **for**-ist) Forest on mountain slopes.

Mucus (**myoo**-kuhss) A slimy substance that is secreted by glands in the mucous membrane as a protective lubricant coating.

Mummify (**muh**-muh-fye) To embalm and dry the body of an animal after death according to the practice of the ancient Egyptians.

Mutation (myoo-**tay**-shuhn) A sudden alteration from the parent type, caused by a change in a gene resulting in a new characteristic.

Nectar (**nek**-tur) A sweet liquid secreted by the flowers of various plants.

Nocturnal (nok-**tur**-nuhl) Active at night rather than during the day.

Nurse (**nurss**) To suckle milk from the mammary glands of a mother.

Omnivore (**om**-nuh-vor) An animal that eats everything, both animal and plant matter.

Opposable thumb (uh-**poze**-uh-buhl **thuhm**) A thumb that can be brought together with other fingers on the same hand to grasp an object.

Order (**or**-dur) A category of biological classification between family and class. An order includes related families.

Oxygen (**ok**-suh-juhn) A gas without color, odor, or taste that forms about one fifth of the air and is necessary for the survival of animals and plants.

Phylum (**fye**-luhm) [plural, **Phyla** (**fye**-lah)] The most inclusive category of biological classification within a kingdom. A phylum includes related classes.

Placental (pluh-**sen**-tuhl) The name given to mammals whose young develop inside the mother's womb.

Plankton (**plangk**-tuhn) Tiny plants or animals that float and drift in water.

Poacher (**pohch**-ur) A person who hunts animals illegally in a forbidden area.

Pod (**pod**) A group of seals or whales.

Pollen (**pol**-uhn) The fine, powderlike material produced by flowering plants, and functioning as the male element in fertilization.

Predators (**pred**-uh-tors) Animals that chase, kill, and eat other animals.

Prehensile tail (pree-**hen**-sil tayl) A tail, found in some primates and marsupials, that is specially adapted for grasping and support.

Prey (**pray**) A creature hunted or caught for food.

Primates (**prye**-mayts) An order of animals with grasping hands and flexible feet. The order includes humans, apes, and monkeys.

Primatologist (prye-muh-**tol**-uh-jist) A person skilled in the study of the origin, structure, development, and behavior of primates.

Prosimians (proh-**sim**-ee-uhns) Of or belonging to the Prosimii, a suborder of primates that includes the lemurs, lorises, and tarsiers.

Retina (**ret**-in-uh) The sensory membrane in the back of the eye that receives the image formed by the eye's lens.

Ruminant (**roo**-muh-nuhnt) Any of various hoofed, even-toed mammals, such as cattle, having a stomach that is divided into several compartments and chewing a cud of regurgitated, partially digested food.

Savanna (suh-**van**-uh) A flat grassland of tropical or subtropical regions.

Scent (**sent**) A distinctive odor produced by the glands of an animal.

Scent marking (**sent mar**-king) Urinary marks made by a male mammal to outline his personal territory; meant to keep others out.

Semi-aquatic (**sem**-ee-uh-**kwaw**-tik) Adapted for living in or near water; not entirely aquatic.

Social animals (**soh**-shuhl an-uh-muhls) Animals that live in an organized group.

Species (**spee**-sees) The most specific category of biological classification. A species includes organisms that are similar and can breed only among themselves.

Steppe (**step**) A vast, semi-arid, grass-covered plain, usually lightly wooded, as found in southeastern Europe, Central Asia, and Siberia.

Teat (**teet**) The nipple of a female's breast or udder, from which the young suckle milk.

Threatened (**thret**-uhnd) A species that is close to being endangered.

Understory (**uhn**-dur-stor-ee) In the rain forest, the layer of vegetation that is below the canopy and is cooler and more humid than the canopy.

Ungulates (**uhn**-gyuh-layts) Hoofed mammals, including horses, cattle, deer, and antelopes.

Vertebrate (**vur**-tuh-brate) An animal having a backbone or spinal column.

Vulnerable (**vuhl**-nur-uh-buhl) A rare species that should be watched closely to prevent extinction.

Warm-blooded (**worm-bluhd**-id) Able to maintain a constant body temperature, no matter what the surrounding temperature is.

Zoologist (zoo-**ol**-uh-jist) A person who studies the biological science of animals.

Index

Index

Time-Life Education, Inc. is a division of Time Life Inc.

TIME LIFE INC.

PRESIDENT and CEO: George Artandi
CHIEF OPERATING OFFICER: Mary Davis Holt

TIME-LIFE EDUCATION, INC.
PRESIDENT: Mary Davis Holt

MANAGING EDITOR: Mary J. Wright

Time-Life Student Library
MAMMALS

EDITOR: Karin Kinney

Deputy Editor: Terrell Smith
Text Editor: Allan Fallow
Associate Editor/Research and Writing: Mary Saxton
Picture Coordinator: Lisa Groseclose
Page Makeup Specialist: Monika D. Lynde
Technical Artist: John Drummond

Designed by: Phillip Unetic and Lori Cohen, 3r1 Group

Special Contributors: Sara Mark (development), Patricia Daniels, Marilyn Terrell, Barry Wolverton (text), Catherine Tyson (research), Barbara Klein (index).
Copyeditor: Darcie Johnston
Correspondents: Maria Vincenza Aloisi (Paris), Christine Hinze (London), Christina Lieberman (New York).

Vice President of Marketing and Publisher: Rosalyn McPherson Andrews
Vice President of Sales: Robert F. Sheridan
Director of Book Production: Patricia Pascale
Director of Publishing Technology: Betsi McGrath
Director of Photography and Research: John Conrad Weiser
Marketing Manager: Michele Stegmaier
Production Manager: Carolyn M. Clark
Quality Assurance Manager: James King
Chief Librarian: Louise D. Forstall
Direct Marketing Consultant: Barbara Erlandson

Consultants:

Dr. George Watson is former curator of birds and chairman of the Department of Vertebrate Zoology in the Smithsonian Institution's National Museum of Natural History. He is an authority on seabirds and serves on the Committee for Research and Exploration of the National Geographic Society. He is the author of Birds of the Antarctic and Sub-Antarctic.

David Dudgeon is Professor of Ecology and Biodiversity at the University of Hong Kong. He specializes in stream biology and wildlife conservation in Asia. His work includes ecological studies and matters relating to wildlife conservation, working alongside such organizations as the World Wide Fund for Nature (HK) and the Agriculture and Fisheries Department of the Hong Kong Government.

Dr. Gerhard Hartmann is Professor of Zoology at the University of Hamburg, Germany. His main area of research is the study of marine mammals, both fossil and recent, and problems of zoogeography and paleozoogeography. He has worked as a consultant with many nature conservation associations.

Andrea Courduvelis is a teacher at Lyles Crouch Elementary School in Alexandria, Va. She is currently teaching gifted children in grades 3 to 5 and is an instructional leader in the AIMS (Activities Integrating Math and Science) program to train teachers and principals to effectively use AIMS materials.

Sean Duffy is a fifth grade teacher at Flint Hill Elementary School in Fairfax County, Va. He has been active in curriculum development and teacher training for 17 years and is the recipient of numerous grants and teaching awards, including the Virginia Museum of Natural History's Thomas Jefferson medal for "outstanding contributions to natural science education," and has twice been a state-level finalist in NSTA's Presidential Awards in Science Teaching.

Third printing 1999. Printed in U.S.A.
School and library distribution by Time-Life Education, P.O. Box 85026, Richmond, Virginia 23285-5026.
Telephone: 1-800-449-2010
Internet: WWW.TIMELIFEEDU.COM

TIME-LIFE is a trademark of Time Warner Inc. U.S.A.

Library of Congress Cataloging-in-Publication Data
Mammals.
    128 pp.   1.7 cm. — (Time-Life student library)
    Includes index.
    Summary: Describes the eating habits, defenses, parenting, and social behavior of mammals.
        ISBN 0-7835-1351-8
        1. Mammals—Juvenile literature. [1. Mammals.] I. Time-Life Books. II. Series.
    QL706.2.M345 1997
599—dc21   97-28565
                                                                    CIP
                                                                    AC

R 10 9 8 7 6 5 4 3 2 1

OTHER PUBLICATIONS

TIME-LIFE KIDS
Library of First Questions and Answers
A Child's First Library of Learning
I Love Math
Nature Company Discoveries
Understanding Science & Nature

HISTORY
Our American Century
World War II
What Life Was Like
The American Story
Voices of the Civil War
The American Indians
Lost Civilizations
Mysteries of the Unknown
Time Frame
The Civil War
Cultural Atlas

SCIENCE/NATURE
Voyage Through the Universe

DO IT YOURSELF
Total Golf
How to Fix It
The Time-Life Complete Gardener
Home Repair and Improvement
The Art of Woodworking

COOKING
Weight Watchers®, Smart Choice
Recipe Collection
Great Taste-Low Fat
Williams-Sonoma Kitchen Library

For information on and a full description of any of the Time-Life Books series listed above, please call 1-800-621-7026 or write:

Reader Information
Time-Life Customer Service
P.O. Box C-32068
Richmond, Virginia 23261-2068